loving robert lowell

sandra hochman

loving robert lowell

TURNER

Turner Publishing Company
Nashville, Tennessee
New York, New York

www.turnerpublishing.com

Loving Robert Lowell

Cover design: Maddie Cothren
Book design: Glen Edelstein

Library of Congress Cataloging-in-Publication Data

Names: Hochman, Sandra, author.
Loving Robert Lowell / Sandra Hochman.
Nashville, Tennessee : Turner Publishing Company, [2017]
LCCN 2017002565 | ISBN 9781683365372 (pbk. : alk. paper)
LCC PS3558.O34 L68 2017 | DDC 813/.54--dc23
LC record available at https://lccn.loc.gov/2017002565

9781683365372

Printed in the United States of America
16 17 18 19 20 9 8 7 6 5 4 3 2 1

For my beautiful friend
Emily McAllister

loving robert lowell

1

Cal

It was spring of 1961. I had found a part-time job. Then something fortuitous happened. My friend and literary mentor, James T. Farrell, suggested I interview Robert Lowell for *Encounter* magazine. I knew *Encounter* was a prestigious magazine in London where Stephen Spender and many other literary people wrote interviews and articles and published poetry. James T. Farrell had "pull" with Mr. Lasky, the editor. James also knew I needed extra money, and he admired my literary interviews that had been published in some small magazines. He was always generous about helping me publish.

"The Lowells have just moved to New York City from Boston," James said, giving me Robert Lowell's private phone number. "I'm sure Lowell would be flattered to have you interview him. He loves promoting himself, and a lot of people are now talking about his poetry. His book *Life Studies,* which came out last year, was controversial but got such rave reviews. Now that he's almost a mainstream writer, people want to know everything about him, especially in England where Faber & Faber is publishing all his books and T. S. Eliot is his editor and close friend."

"But what makes you think Robert Lowell will talk to me?" I asked.

"Of course he'll talk to you if I tell him to. What man doesn't want to talk to a pretty, young, intellectual interviewer?"

I remember the day I interviewed Robert Lowell. It was a warm and sunny Friday when my boss, Mr. Moss, went out to lunch. I summoned my nerve and dialed the Lowell number that James T. Farrell had given me. I was not really nervous about writing interviews. Interviews for me were like water-color portraits, and I was good at writing them. I remembered that Robert Lowell had been such a gentleman when I met him five years previously in Cambridge. I knew that to write a great interview, one had to be an artist and gently run your brush on the inner life of the person you were talking to. I mused about the inner life of Robert Lowell. What was he really like? I knew he was Catholic and had been a conscientious objector during World War II, but how do you get into the mind of a genius? I was afraid he would say no, but I summoned my courage anyway.

I dialed the number. After a few rings, Robert Lowell answered. I recognized his soft voice with that slight Southern accent from when I had briefly audited his class at Boston University. I said my name. "I hope you remember me," I said shyly into the phone. Then he asked me a surprising question.

"What do you look like?" he asked.

Obviously my name meant nothing to him, and he did not remember me at all. I didn't take this personally. After all, he had taught hundreds of young female students since I had met him in 1955. Silence. I thought for a moment how to answer.

"Well, I'm five foot three, average athletic body, green eyes, blonde and brownish hair."

I was mortified to have to describe myself physically over the phone. I wished I could have told him something more exotic or more literary. Suddenly something clicked in his mind. He now remembered who I was.

"Oh, yes. You're the girl Jim Farrell said was a good poet," he said. I felt relieved. I continued talking. I explained it would be very gracious of him if he allowed me to interview him for an article that James assured me he could place in *Encounter* magazine.

He sounded friendly. There was nothing snobbish or conceited about Robert Lowell. In fact, he seemed very modest. I held his voice to my ear. It was thrilling. It was as if I were light years away from him, but through the black magic of copper wire, he was speaking through my ear into my soul. My heart was now beating fast.

"And where will this interview take place?" he asked me with unexpected interest and enthusiasm.

I wasn't expecting this question. I immediately thought, "Oh my God, what restaurant can I invite him to? I'm broke." And then I remembered that Mr. Sidney Kaye, the good-natured owner of the Russian Tea Room, right up the block from Mr. Moss's office, allowed me to sign a tab. Mr. Kaye, thank God, liked me enough to give me credit. I had been a regular at the Russian Tea Room ever since I was a student at Bennington.

"The Russian Tea Room?" I said tentatively.

"I love the Russian Tea Room," he said in a booming voice.

"Do you have any time next week?" I asked.

"Next week? How about now? I can take a cab and be there in half an hour. Is that all right?"

I was taken aback by the immediacy of his acceptance and availability. I imagined such an important writer and professor would be too busy to see me so soon.

"I'll be there," I said. "I'll be waiting for you."

I ran into Mr. Moss's bathroom, combed my hair, put on some lipstick, changed from my work sneakers to high heels, and ran up the block to the Tea Room. As I sat in the fabled Russian Tea Room with my notebook, I thought about everything I knew about Robert Lowell so that I could think up some appropriate questions to ask him. Of course I had read every poem he ever published. I also knew he was a Boston Brahmin, a Lowell, who rebelled against his aristocratic and uptight background. I had memorized many poems from *Lord Weary's Castle,* his book that won the Pulitzer Prize when he was thirty. I knew he had been married to Jean Stafford, the excellent novelist, who wrote *Boston Adventure,* and he was now married to the novelist Elizabeth Hardwick, who everyone called "Lizzie." I knew he was a genius. I knew he had been a conscientious objector during World War II. I knew he had gone to Harvard for just one year and then switched to Kenyon to be near the critic and poet John Crowe Ransom, who was his mentor. Most of all, I had read *Land of Unlikeness,* his first slim volume of poems which later became *Lord Weary's Castle,* and I knew that he was a compulsive reviser of all his work. I also knew that his early poems were religious as he searched to find God, and I had identified with them because at the time that I first read them, and even now, I too was on a search to find the divine meaning of life. I knew he was now forty-three.

The Russian Tea Room was the hangout for the well-heeled crowd of actors, agents, and people in the musical world. I used to go there after concerts at Carnegie Hall with my first husband from whom I was separated, Ivry, and sometimes for lunch. Now at lunchtime well-known artists and their handlers were coming through the glass revolving door. It seemed to me that everyone was successful and upbeat. The Tea Room had the aura of a million deals and conversations that took place there in the leather booths or at the closely placed tables. There were

4

murals of ballerinas and naked women on the walls painted by the painter Blatos, a charming older Russian man with a cigarette holder who usually hung out in the restaurant talking to the owner and eyeing the young women with his huge watery brown eyes. Mr. Kaye never took down the Christmas ornaments on the chandelier, so at the Russian Tea Room it was eternally Christmas.

I was sitting and waiting for my interview in a red leather booth in the front of the restaurant, staring at the colorful Christmas balls on the chandeliers. I looked at my watch. Mr. Lowell was already ten minutes late. Was he really coming to meet me, or had he, at the last minute, changed his mind?

Soon the disheveled Robert Lowell came spinning through the revolving glass doors looking for me. He certainly didn't look his age of forty-three. Because of his smile he seemed younger. There was something boyish in his walk. He was tall and fit, he looked like someone who was not an intellectual but might be a professional athlete. He instantly waved when he saw me and seemed to recognize me as he checked his tweed coat at the cloakroom. I had forgotten how good-looking he was. He was wearing thick black-framed glasses, a blue cashmere sweater vest, a pair of corduroy Brooks Brothers pants, and moccasins. He came over to where I was sitting and instantly sat down next to me in the red leather booth as if he had known me forever. Gregory, the Russian waiter wearing the Cossack uniform that was part of the Russian Tea Room's attempt at old-world Russian authenticity, came over to my table. Gregory was a short man with chubby cheeks and a big smile. He and I, over the years, had become friends. I always chatted with Gregory.

"Gregory, this is the greatest living American poet, Robert Lowell. I'm going to interview him right here at your table," I said in a cheerful voice.

Gregory smiled. Robert Lowell seemed flattered that I

5

thought of him in such an exalted way. Gregory took his drink order for a vodka martini and my order for a ginger ale.

We began talking. Suddenly our casual conversation stopped and Robert Lowell blurted out: "I'm leaving Lizzie."

I was a bit shocked by this sudden personal confession. I knew Lizzie was Elizabeth Hardwick, his blond, attractive, Southern wife. As far as I knew, he was happily married, but I didn't know much about his personal life.

"You mean you're leaving your wife?" I asked, slightly stunned.

James T. Farrell had not informed me of this piece of literary gossip when he suggested the interview. It was certainly a shock. For a moment, I went back in my memory to the time I was a sophomore at Bennington College. I had discovered *Lord Weary's Castle* as a fledgling poet. I was impressed by the magnificent language, rhyme, subject matter, passion, and pure genius of every single line in his book which I thought was a masterpiece. It was at Bennington that Robert Lowell and Lizzie had come up to the College for him to give a reading to the small, all-female student body. He was a huge success reading in the "Carriage Barn" from *Lord Weary's Castle* and *Mills of the Kavanaughs.* Dozens of young women gathered around him after the reading with copies of his books for him to sign. They were all flirtatious. I was too shy to meet him. I noticed his wife was smiling, but I sensed she was none too happy with the pretty, young female literary groupies who were two decades younger than she was and eagerly demanding Robert Lowell's attention. I was briefly introduced to Mr. and Mrs. Lowell at a luncheon given by the college president, Fred Burkhardt. I had been invited to the luncheon because I was one of the co-editors of *Silo,* the Bennington literary magazine. I remember thinking that Mrs. Lowell was very attractive. She was elegantly dressed. She had the charm and accent of a Southern belle.

Now, I was sitting next to Robert Lowell, many years after that poetry reading at Bennington, and he was confiding to me that he was leaving his wife. I felt sad to hear this news. I just sat and listened to the great poet speak to me about his private life. I wanted to console him.

"Oh, I feel sorry for you, Mr. Lowell, and for Mrs. Lowell."

He ordered another vodka martini and, for me, another ginger ale.

"Don't feel sorry for us. I'm happy. I've wanted to start a new life for at least a year and we both know our marriage is over, but now we will always be friends. No more confrontations and arguments for me. Lizzie feels the same way."

"To tell you the truth I'm just newly separated from my husband, and I know it's very painful to leave someone you once loved. Are you sure you can't patch things up?" I asked sympathetically.

"I'm sure, my dear. And I've been sure for a long time. It's better to live alone than to be constantly at each other's throat. I've already made arrangements to have an apartment of my own."

"Oh, really? You found an apartment so quickly? Where is it?"

"It's on the Upper East Side." He sounded a bit vague. "I don't plan to live there permanently, but it's perfect for the time being."

I felt uncomfortable hearing about his private life. I just wanted to begin the interview.

"Tell me about your book *Imitations*," I said.

I took out my pen and interview notebook so I could begin asking him more questions about his work and his influences.

"I don't want to talk about my work. This is not the right time to be interviewing me," he said.

"I'm sorry," I said. "Perhaps we can do this at another time when you are less distraught."

He changed the subject. I think he was afraid I was going to leave the restaurant.

"Don't leave, please don't go, I need to talk to someone. I

remember you sitting in my creative writing class several years ago at Boston University. Jim seems very fond of your work. I'm happy to be with a young poet. I'm at loose ends." He put his hand on my hand. "Put away your notebook," he said. "I want to know you."

He ordered another vodka martini. I was still sipping my ginger ale. He then suggested we order lunch. Gregory came to take our order.

"May I order for you?" he asked.

"Yes, Mr. Lowell," I said.

"Oh, for God sakes, don't call me Mr. Lowell, call me Cal; that's what all my friends call me."

The man I was from then on to call "Cal" ordered black caviar blinis for both of us, the most expensive dish on the menu. I was now praying that he would pick up the check. Robert Lowell now held my hand and moved closer to me in the leather booth. I could tell he was having a good time.

"Do you mind if I nickname you Butterball?" he asked.

It was a strange request and sort of embarrassing. I blushed. That would not have been the nickname I chose for myself, but what the hell. The black caviar blinis arrived. We both poured melted butter over the stack of thin pancakes covered with black caviar and sour cream. We began eating. Cal ordered himself another vodka martini.

"How did you get the nickname Cal?" I asked.

"At boarding school. St. Marks. I'm nicknamed after Caligula. You see, I was a bit of a bully myself. Somewhere in my fantasy I wanted to be a tyrant. I loved to give orders. Even when I was a little boy in Boston my mother used to call me 'her little Napoleon,' but I liked Caligula better than Napoleon. I would much rather be named after a tyrant than, say, Abraham Lincoln. I'm a better Cal than an Abe." He stopped talking about himself and started asking me questions.

8

"Are you still a poet?" he asked.

"Of course. I'm a writer for the rest of my life. My first book of poems, *Voyage Home,* was published last year in Paris by Anaïs Nin. It's published in English and has a blurb by Alastair Reid."

"Alastair Reid? That's impressive. He's a good poet. Then, we are two poets."

Cal became suddenly romantic. But I had been around artists all my adult life and I knew that most male artists were big flirts, so I didn't take Cal seriously.

"I love being with you," he said passionately.

"I like being with you too, Cal," I said.

"I have a secret to tell you," he said, now whispering in my ear.

"Tell me," I said, laughing.

I could smell his Bay Rum cologne as he came closer to me. I knew the odor because I once bought the same cologne for my father when I was vacationing in St. Thomas. I now felt intoxicated by the aroma.

"I'm about to change my life. I'm not happy. And I want to start all over again," he said with finality. "I've been miserable. I want a new life."

I had been desperately miserable myself, but I didn't say so. I was tired of the old life that I had created for myself which I saw now as a mistake. I wanted to slip out of my identity of Mrs. Gitlis the way one slips out of a pair of old bedroom slippers. I, too, wanted a new life.

"What do you mean by a new life, Cal?" I asked.

I was almost twenty years younger than he was and suddenly I thought he might actually be Lord Weary. He seemed to be weary of being Robert Lowell.

"Listen, I want you to listen to me," Cal said. "I want you to believe me. You're exactly the woman I've been looking for all my life and never could find. You're a poet. You're young. You're beautiful. And you attract me. I want my new life to be with you. Love happens quickly. And it is happening for me.

9

From the second I walked in the revolving door, I looked at you and I knew I could start all over again. Do you know who you look like?"

"Who?" I asked.

"You look like the Russian poet Anna Akhmatova. She's one of my favorite poets, and I want to show you her poetry, which I've translated. Stalin tortured her. Stalin ruined her life as he ruined the lives of so many writers in Russia. You are so much like her. I can't wait to read your poetry," he said.

Everything was happening so quickly. That should have been the first red flag, but it wasn't. I admitted to myself I was attracted to him. He had beautiful cat eyes, yellowish green, and high cheek bones, and I loved his voice. And should I believe him? I felt confused. This was what in Paris they called *coup de foudre*. It was as if a bolt of lightning had hit him and me at the same time.

"Where did you pick up your charming slight Southern accent?" I asked, somewhat embarrassed by this sudden thunderbolt of mutual passion.

"I've had this accent ever since I was a boy at St. Marks School. And then I lived in the South, so it stuck. But I don't want to talk about my accent. I want to talk about us."

It was all very mysterious. Suddenly I was Alice in Wonderland, with things getting "curiouser and curiouser" just as when Alice fell down the rabbit hole. I had to admit to myself that in this strange wonderland of the Russian Tea Room with Christmas balls hanging above us from the gold chandeliers, even in the beginning of spring, we were both enjoying the moment of mutual attraction and flirtation.

"But Cal, I don't even know you. Just your poetry," I said. "But aren't you still living with your wife? James told me you're living on Riverside Drive."

"I'm not living with her anymore. Tomorrow I'm moving everything into my new apartment. I want to get a divorce.

I'll be living in my own apartment in a day. I just used my trust fund to buy a co-op on Sixty-Seventh Street near Central Park for Lizzie, who will be very happy living there with our daughter Harriet. She's a darling, my daughter, and I know you'll love her. But of course I'll be living alone in my new apartment, and you might come visit me. I'm thrilled at the idea that I'm now a single man."

Cal called for the check. I wondered if he was serious; but it seemed very believable to me that he had already left his wife. I was relieved that he was separated, and I was separated, and who knew what could happen?

"Where are you living now that you're not living with your wife?" I asked.

"I'm staying with a cousin. Let's get out of here," he said, and left a huge tip after paying the check.

He tipped the hat-check woman, who smiled seductively at this tall handsome man, retrieving his old coat and professor's briefcase. Cal grabbed my arm. We went outside. He hailed a cab. Once we were in the cab, he said to the cab driver, "Take us to the Brooklyn Bridge, please."

"Why are we going there?" I asked him.

"I want to read Hart Crane's poem 'To the Brooklyn Bridge' to you, right on the Brooklyn Bridge."

That sounded so romantic. Two poets on the Brooklyn Bridge reading Hart Crane. He took a first edition of Hart Crane's collected poems out of his briefcase to show me.

"Hart Crane is one of my favorite poets," I said breathlessly.

How well I knew the tragic life of Hart Crane. I had studied his life and work while still in boarding school. He had been born into a wealthy family in Garrettsville, Ohio. His father had made a fortune selling chocolate bars. But his father turned his back on him and refused to help support him. He worked for a while in his father's factory, but he hated it. His life was so tragic, the way many poet's lives unfortunately are. I'm

11

sure it didn't help that he was tormented sexually. Hart Crane had tried to have a love affair with Peggy Cowley, the wife of Malcolm Cowley, the critic and poet and now an editor at Viking Press. She left her husband for him, but Hart Crane couldn't stop picking up sailors so she left him. After that disastrous affair with Mrs. Cowley, Hart Crane booked himself on a cargo ship to Mexico. He jumped off the back of the ship into the ice-cold ocean, committing suicide. His body was never found. This was in 1932. Hart Crane left behind many poems. The most touching poem was *The Bridge,* which I had read and related to as one of the most heartbreaking of modern poems. While I was thinking about Hart Crane during our taxi ride, Cal said:

"Yes, I'm going to rent an apartment on East End Avenue immediately, and you will always be with me."

As we got out of the cab, I said, "I don't think that's possible right now."

"Why not?"

"I haven't told you. I'm still married, to a concert violinist, Ivry Gitlis. We're on a trial separation, but I'm sure I'm no longer in love with him and we're going to get a divorce. In fact, I'm planning to divorce him this summer. But I'm definitely living with my father until then."

As we walked on the Brooklyn Bridge, Cal didn't seem to hear me, talking gently to me and holding my hand.

"Of course we will both get a divorce. You can visit me, and soon you won't ever want to leave me." Cal said.

He seemed very sure of himself. I wasn't as sure about this escapade as he was. I thought that being so good-looking and well-mannered and rich and famous had made it easy for him to attract women to his side. Suddenly live with him? This all seemed dreamlike and impossible. I wasn't sure I was ready for a love affair. But that afternoon I knew I was having a great time. I felt exalted, as if I were in the middle of a romantic Russian film. I was, after all, spending time with America's greatest poet, and he seemed to care for me. I felt elated. Although I hadn't had anything to drink, I felt high. My mind was racing. What if all this was real? I had never been romantically involved for very long with any other man but Ivry. Perhaps Cal's new life would be mine also, and I could finally find the happiness that eluded me in my four-year marriage and six-year relationship with Ivry. In fact, happiness had eluded me my whole life, especially in my childhood, which kept me away from my parents for nine years at a boarding school, longing for love and a family I could be with. Was I mad? Was he mad? Were we two mad people falling in love? Was this a *folie à deux*? All my life I had this empty hole in my soul because I had been so different from what my parents expected me to be. Writing poetry constantly made me so different from other people. I was always translating every experience into a poem. I admired the poetry of Saint Theresa of Avila, who was originally Jewish but converted to Catholicism and eventually became a nun. Her poems were outcries of a desire to be one with God. Her closest friend was also a poet, Saint John of the Cross, who became a monk. Was I Saint Theresa who had met my Saint John of the Cross? Saint John of the Cross had written a great book of Catholic poetry, *The Dark Night of the Soul*. All of this went through my mind. But there was no darkness now, only a burst of light because I was deliriously happy. It started to snow—a light spring snow. The snowflakes fell on Cal's black hair and dark eyelashes. He was sparkling with snowflakes. It was such a lovely moment.

"I'm never going to leave you," Cal said and kissed me.

After the long kiss, we began walking to the bridge, holding hands. It all seemed natural, as if it were the beginning of our new life. We seemed to be walking on a bridge to a new world. I felt a surge of happiness. Was it possible I had died and gone to heaven?

"This poem, 'To Brooklyn Bridge,' expresses the ecstasy and vision of Hart Crane's lost soul," Cal said.

He began reading to me from the book:

How many dawns, chill from his rippling rest
The seagull's wings shall dip and pivot him,
Shedding white rings of tumult, building high
Over the chained bay waters Liberty—

Then, with inviolate curve, forsake our eyes
As apparitional as sails that cross
Some page of figures to be filed away;
—Till elevators drop us from our day . . .

I think of cinemas, panoramic sleights
With multitudes bent toward some flashing scene
Never disclosed, but hastened to again,
Foretold to other eyes on the same screen;

And Thee, across the harbor, silver-paced
As though the sun took step of thee, yet left
Some motion ever unspent in thy stride,—
Implicitly thy freedom staying thee!

Out of some subway scuttle, cell or loft
A bedlamite speeds to thy parapets,
Tilting there momently, shrill shirt ballooning,
A jest falls from the speechless caravan.

Down Wall, from girder into street noon leaks,
A rip-tooth of the sky's acetylene;
All afternoon the cloud-flown derricks turn . . .
Thy cables breathe the North Atlantic still.

And obscure as that heaven of the Jews,
Thy guerdon . . . Accolade thou dost bestow

14

Of anonymity time cannot raise:
Vibrant reprieve and pardon thou dost show.

O harp and altar, of the fury fused,
(How could mere toil align thy choiring strings!)
Terrific threshold of the prophet's pledge,
Prayer of pariah, and the lover's cry,——

Again the traffic lights that skim thy swift
Unfractioned idiom, immaculate sigh of stars,
Beading thy path—condense eternity:
And we have seen night lifted in thine arms.

Under thy shadow by the piers I waited;
Only in darkness is thy shadow clear.
The City's fiery parcels all undone,
Already snow submerges an iron year . . .

O Sleepless as the river under thee,
Vaulting the sea, the prairies' dreaming sod,
Unto us lowliest sometime sweep, descend
And of the curveship lend a myth to God.

When he finished reading, Cal switched roles from the romantic lover to the brilliant professor. He was now a man sharing his passion for the work of Hart Crane, but I felt he was also using this poem to woo me.

"I'm enthralled by the way even something as fundamentally stationary as a bridge, with Hart Crane's talent, becomes a moving object," Cal said. "There is a delicate balance that Crane manages to strike between the divine and industrial." Cal seemed to get lost in his own thoughts for a moment. Suddenly he hugged me. "I want to marry you," he said.

We kissed each other again and held each other for a long time. It was almost as if Cal were trying to imaginatively connect fantasy with reality. After the kiss, we just stared at each other. Then we began walking in the snowflakes, away from the Brooklyn Bridge, in silence.

Back in Manhattan, Cal hailed a cab.

"Where are we going?" I asked.

I was so vulnerable. I wanted love so badly. But could it be that he loved me too? Was that possible? Could I really be as fortunate to find the man of my dreams? Could it be that my luck was changing, and that I was now experiencing real love for the first time in my life?

"We're going to the Carlyle Hotel to make love," Cal said spontaneously. "I don't take possession of my apartment until the day after tomorrow, and I don't want to bring you back to my cousin's house. I don't want anyone to know about us just yet."

"Are you sure you're telling me the truth? The number that James Farrell gave me to contact you for the interview, he said was your home. Are you sure you are living with your cousin?"

"Of course I am. I was just picking up and packing my clothes, which I've been doing for the past week. I swear to you on the life of my child, I'm not a liar; everything I'm telling you is true. You must believe me; why would I lie to you? I'm a very honorable person. I left Riverside Drive days ago."

Now I felt relieved. And why not? This was turning into a romantic adventure. When we arrived at the Carlyle Hotel, and stood at the registration desk, I suddenly saw panic on Cal's face. He started to sweat.

"What's wrong?" I asked. I thought he was about to pass out. He whispered to me, "I just saw my editor Roger Straus going to dinner in the restaurant with some of our friends from Boston. Let's get out of here."

I could tell that our new liaison had to be secretive, and that Cal was nervous of word getting out about what I now felt was our love affair. The concierge had a phony French accent.

"Yes, my dear sir, can I help you? You want to rent a room?" he asked Cal.

"Let's go," Cal said to me.

Cal paid no attention to the concierge. We walked out of the Carlyle Hotel as quickly as possible. The concierge was left looking startled. Outside the side entrance to the hotel, there were several limousines parked, waiting for customers. I was lifted out of my own life now, feeling somewhat delirious, as if I were drunk on our sexual attraction.

He spoke to one of the drivers. "Please take us to the Plaza," Cal said. Then he changed his mind once we were seated in the back of the limousine, thinking he might also run into people he knew at the Plaza. "Take us to the Gotham Hotel."

The driver agreed. Cal told the driver that he might not be leaving until early in the morning. When we arrived I saw that Cal gave him a $100 bill and asked him to wait.

"Very good," the driver said politely.

The sun was setting. I felt as if I were living inside a dream. I was with the most brilliant man on earth, and perhaps the most handsome. I was about to make love with him. I felt as if I were stepping into the sunrise of a new life. I was so happy. "Please let this be true," I said to myself. How could such a fabulous man be interested in me? Was it because I reminded him of a Russian poet? Although he was so much older than I was, he seemed to need my care and my love. I was ready to follow him anywhere. I just wanted to be near him, to smell him and touch him and hold him. My whole body was on fire. I knew that sex was the glue that kept people together. Not money, not fame, not even family. Would our attraction fuse together in just one night? It was difficult to predict the longevity of our sexual delirium. But it wouldn't only be sex. It would be sex and adoration. Robert Lowell was like a god, my literary hero at Bennington, and now I was going to experience him in a whole new and beautiful physical way. What would it be like? I was nervous and ecstatic at the same time. Would I disappoint him? I felt cold and hot simultaneously. Cal checked us into the charmingingly old and small Gotham Hotel under the name of Mr. and Mrs. Hart Crane. The man at the desk didn't ask any questions, and Cal asked for the key to our suite. The hotel was real. Cal was real. But was this really happening?

As we walked down the long hotel hallway and into the room, we both felt sexually excited. There was a huge bed with a chintz bedspread. There were magazines laid out on a coffee table. Cal and I stood hugging each other.

"I don't think we will be reading magazines," Cal said, and we both laughed.

Eagerly we both took off our clothes without any embarrassment. I looked at Cal nude. He was sculpted perfectly. I loved his tall body with curly black hairs on his chest. I loved his very white skin. He could have posed for the statue of David in Florence. Despite the fact that he had nicknamed me Butterball, Cal seemed to also love my body and whispered "You are so beautiful" in my ear. Soon we were in bed. Before we made love, for a moment, I imagined that we were riding on a raft down the waters of the Amazon River. I could hear all the jungle sounds, the cawing of the birds, the buzzing of dragonflies, the screams of owls and monkeys, while the huge bright moon shone on our bodies. As I lay back in Cal's arms, I felt safe. Our legs and arms intertwined. Were we two poets madly in love? We could not stop making love.

I lay inside my imaginary jungle peacefully until early in the morning. The car Cal had hired was still waiting for us downstairs. The driver opened the door for us to enter. We sat in the back of the car holding hands. We still had that erotic feeling that we had felt when making love to each other. I felt that his cologne was all over my body. He was touching my hair and my face, and I could hear his breath. I had never felt this way before, not even about my husband. The limousine arrived in front of my father's apartment at 929 Park Avenue at nine in the morning.

"I don't even know your phone number at your father's apartment or in your office," Cal said.

I wrote out both numbers on a page I tore out of my notebook and gave it to him. He kissed that paper, folded it carefully, and put it in his pocket. So much for the interview.

"I'm going to quit my job working for Mr. Moss," I said. "And just study and spend time with you. I have enough savings that I can afford to do that."

"You are?" He seemed pleased with my decision.

"Yes. I'll still go to Columbia Graduate School a few afternoons a week and attend the Actors Studio Playwrights Unit. Other than that, Cal, I want to spend as much time with you as possible. I want this dream to last. I don't want this feeling of Eros to ever go away. And I want you to try writing plays as well as poetry; I know there's a great playwright inside you."

"Oh, I've always wanted to write plays. This is wonderful. I see how good you are for me. What's the Actors Studio Playwrights Unit?" he asked.

We were standing on the street while strangers passed us going to work or walking their dogs.

"It's a group of playwrights who get together once a week and hear their plays read by actors from the studio. You should come with me."

We were holding on to each other in the early morning.

"I should. Perhaps this will inspire me to write plays," Cal said.

"It will."

"I want to spend all my time with you, too," Cal said. "You inspire me. I feel as if I have now entered our new, exciting life. I can't wait to pack my bags and leave my cousin's apartment. We'll have a place where we can be together."

We continued holding each other.

"Will I meet your cousin?" I asked.

"Of course you'll meet my cousin. Now that I'm a single man, we can do all these beautiful things that I wanted to do in New York. I have a part-time job teaching at the New School, but I want to do a lot more than teach and write. I want to go with you to the opera, and see ballet and modern dance."

It seemed amazing to me that five months earlier, I had been in Paris in an unhappy marriage, and now a whole new life could be opening to me with the great poet, the man whom I had secretly loved by reading his poetry, and now it was that very poet who claimed he was in love with me. Our lovemaking at the Gotham Hotel had been heated, passionate and beyond the boundaries of anything I had ever experienced sexually. But could I really believe him? What made him think he could change his life so easily? We parted with a final kiss, and Cal said he would call me later.

Entering the elevator of my father's building, I wasn't sure everything Cal said was true. What if he really loved his wife and just wanted a pretty young girl to go to bed with? This stranger, who was so brilliant and talented and whose poetry had changed American poetry forever, was also a very courteous and sexually attractive man. He had been on the cover of *Time* magazine. Why would he want me? He had the career of one of the great twentieth-century poets, and he was just forty-three and had many years to continue writing. Despite his fame, he was modest and kind. I was twenty-five, impressionable, and at the beginning of my literary career. I had so much to learn from him. He had been the mentor to Sylvia Plath and Anne Sexton. He took female poets seriously and went out of his way to help them achieve publishing success. I suddenly thought of his *Life Studies*, which I had read the previous year in Paris, alone at night by myself, when my husband Ivry was asleep. I found it a remarkable book that, like all Cal's other books, had inspired me. Was he really in a

20

life change, able to start a new life with me? And as much as I was attracted to him, was he really someone I could live with? I had made one mistake; I didn't want to make another but the following lines of Robert's had haunted me in Paris before I went to sleep, and before I really knew him:

Now Paris, our black classic, breaking up
Like killer kings on an Etruscan cup.

2

Back Story of a Love Affair

Sadly for my father, who never went past third grade and looked down on artists, but happily for me, I was born a poet. If it wasn't totally in my genes, it certainly was in my excellent education. My mother, Mae, a beautiful woman, who was often compared to Ingrid Bergman, a schoolteacher with a master's degree from Columbia, saw to it that at the age of two I went to the Master's Institute for the Arts, housed in a large art-deco building on 103rd Street, near Riverside Drive. I was sent there by my mother to study eurhythmics, that is to say, rhythm. Since rhythm was my first introduction to learning, clapping my little hands to a tom-tom beat, I am sure eurhythmics got into my blood and influenced my future writing. Poetry is at least 50 percent rhythms.

After my parents' messy divorce, where I was introduced to the agony of the human condition at the age of seven, frequently being fought over in New York City's family court for custody, I was sent, quite unwillingly, to Cherry Lawn Boarding School. Cherry Lawn was a progressive boarding school that emphasized the arts. At the age of eight when I entered, I was immediately cast by the English and drama teacher, Mr. Burwell—who hailed from London and the Old Vic Theater—as Titania in his lower school production of Shakespeare's *A Midsummer Night's Dream*. As an eight-year-old Titania, I hardly knew the meaning of what I was saying, but I loved the attention, the fantasy of being on stage in a costume, and the beautiful words of Shakespeare. Speaking those words made me happy. Even at the age of eight, sailing on the sea of the rhythms of Shakespeare's iambic pentameter, I was in the ocean of endless and beautiful rhythms of language.

At Cherry Lawn, in the lower school, Mr. Burwell later introduced me to books by many of the modern poets and playwrights. He remained my mentor from when I started in the lower school in third grade to when I ended the upper school in twelfth grade. I graduated with honors at sixteen. Mr. Burwell encouraged me to be a writer when I grew up, fanning my dreams by telling me I was very talented.

While I was in the lower school, Mr. Burwell encouraged me to send away for inexpensive hardcover books from Black-wells, a bookstore in England. All my student allowance was spent on money orders for books I ordered from Blackwells. While other children eagerly lined up at mail time to receive letters, brown laundry cases filled with clean clothes, and forbidden salami and cookies from home, I was lining up to receive Blackwells' copy of *The Complete Works of Christopher Marlowe,* or *The Complete Works of Homer,* or *The Masques of Ben Jonson*. These books came from England in brown paper wrapping with exotically colored English stamps on the package. Each time I received a new book from this magical and inexpensive bookstore, and held my new book close to my heart, it was as if a new world had been put into my hands. I loved books, and Mr. Burwell encouraged all of his precocious English students to read the classics as well as modern plays by Tennessee Williams, T. S. Eliot, or García Lorca. At boarding school, I dreamt of growing up to be an artist. But what kind of artist? Painter? Dancer? Actress? Musician? Poet? I loved all these things. Inspired by Mr. Burwell, as well as the art teachers, the music teachers, and the dance instructors, I became a Renaissance Child.

"You know a lot about books, but you know nothing about life," my dad said.

"But daddy," I said, "Books are life."

Later, as a student at a small girl's college, Bennington, I began publishing my poetry in literary magazines, encouraged by my new mentor, the poet Howard Nemerov. My first poems appeared in *Voices, Poetry, Audience,* and other small literary publications. Mr. Nemerov told me he was very proud of my talent and entered two of my poems, without my knowing it, in the *New World Writing* magazine contest for college poets, edited by Donald Hall. My poem "Silence" won. I was honored to be one of the five college poets in the United States to appear in *New World Writing,* which was sold not only to arcane intellectuals who read small literary magazines but to a mass-market public. *New World Writing* was a new kind of mainstream paperback magazine that was really a book with a stitched cover and was sold in large bookstores. When I saw my name in print above a small biography, I was secretly enchanted that this person they were writing about was me. That began my desire to keep publishing. I was hooked.

By the time I re-met Robert Lowell, I had lived in Paris with my concert violinist husband, I was getting a divorce, and I had my first volume of poetry, *Voyage Home,* published in Paris by Two Cities Press in English. *Voyage Home* appeared only because Anaïs Nin and her friend, the writer Lawrence

Durrell, paid Two Cities Press to bring it out. Anaïs Nin was my angel and took me under her literary wing in Paris. My book was a slim volume with a blue and white cover, limited to a hundred copies. It had a rather sad picture of me on the back cover. Under my picture was a blurb by the poet Alastair Reid that appeared without his name. Alastair had taught at Sarah Lawrence, and I had met him in Madrid. Before my book was released, he offered me his distinguished recommendation. He said it was customary to have a quote from another poet, and he would be only too happy to write one for me. He wrote:

"*Voyage Home* is wonderfully clear and shining and very unlike anything else. These poems are a way of looking and, as far as the imagery goes, marvelously consistent, full of color and happenings and living things. These poems move, not rationally, but with a curious, unique logic of feeling."

When Alastair bought my book a few months later at the book-signing party that Anaïs Nin gave for me at the English bookstore in Paris, Alastair did not understand why I used his quote but did not give him credit for the words he had so generously written. I shyly admitted that I was afraid that perhaps the poems weren't very good. I didn't want people to blame him for admiring them if nobody else liked them. He laughed so hard because I was very naïve and, being insecure about my work, was only trying to protect his reputation. I was so innocent about the world of publishing, I didn't know that a "blurb" meant nothing without a well-known writer's name under it.

One of the poems that Alastair liked in *Voyage Home* was called "Asylum of John Claire." John Claire was a mad poet of the nineteenth century in England whose work Howard Nemerov had brought to my attention at Bennington. Looking now at this poem, "Asylum of John Claire," which I wrote in 1960, it seems I could have been writing not about John Claire but Robert Lowell:

Lips hungered, appetite dead
From too much civil wine. Compounding bread
With loaves of silt
John feasted in the green kiln that he built.
"Eternity"whispers the faery fly,
Is not behind the shade of Mary's eye,
"But mixed with breath of angels in the park,
Beneath the burning wing of a skylark."
There, John went fishing mackerel from the sty,
Or looked for Summer in a snowdrop bed.
Mad harmonies were, by the skylark, wed
And strangers came to gape, and so did God.

I had written this poem when I was sixteen in college, portending my appreciation of a madman's genius. But at that time I'd had no idea that I would fall in love with such a madman.

A watercolor portrait that I painted of Robert Lowell now sits in my living room, staring at me. Yes, there he is, every day, smiling at me and my guests through my painting. Looking at that watercolor portrait often makes me remember many of our conversations and incidents in our life together. Our love affair floats back to me like a daydream in watery orange and green. In my portrait, where Robert Lowell wears his sly smile that I grew to love, he appears to be happy.

Although I ended our love affair in a mental ward, my fondness for him as a genius, as well as a courteous and brilliantly humorous man, still remains. I see this now, looking back, how much I learned from him, and how, in many ways, he influenced my own poetry as well as my life. In my favorite book of his poetry, *Imitations*—which is actually a book of free translations of some of his favorite European and Russian poets, published in 1961, the year that our love affair began—I still read over and over his translations made Lowellesque.

The following lines from a poem in *Imitations,* which I often re-read, still feel personal to me, as if he were speaking to me from another place. These are lines from a poem originally written by Baudelaire but imitated by Robert Lowell:

And if the beautiful world less sinister
Had let me live a little longer, I too might have sustained
Your work and brought you comfort,
Seeing how heaven had befriended you.

That *comfort* was not to be.

Ivry Gitlis? I still remember the angry soundscapes of our failing marriage. "I'm tired of you cheating on me," I said. "I want to go to Columbia graduate school and get a master's degree so that maybe, perhaps, one day, in the future, I can earn a living as a college professor."

It was the winter of 1961. I was talking to my soon-to-be ex-husband, Ivry Gitlis, the internationally renowned concert violinist who I felt betrayed our love. We were in New York City for one of his concerts.

"Columbia? Master's degree? Don't be crazy. It's winter. How are you going to get into graduate school?" He scoffed at me, snorting in laughter at my stupid idea.

"Dorothy Butler Farrell said she could get me into the comparative literature masters' program at Columbia University so I could start studying there next week."

"How is she going to do that? With a magic wand?" Ivry asked, sarcastic as usual. His two weapons against me were insults and sarcasm.

"Her family, the Butlers, founded the library, so she has a little pull. She already got me in." I dropped the bomb: "I want a one-year trial separation, Ivry. I want to get a part-time job, I want to go to the Actors Studio where I've been invited into the Playwrights Unit by the director of the unit, Frank

Corsaro, and I want to go to jazz concerts again, give poetry readings, go to galleries, and feel young again. I'm sick of being your full-time baby nurse and manager. I'm tired of being an expat. I miss New York.

"I'm no longer in love with you, Ivry," I added quietly.

That was a dagger to his ego. Ivry, I'm sorry to say, was so conceited, he needed everyone to be in love with him. He needed emotional applause night and day.

"So you've been planning all this behind my back? I need you. I'll never be able to manage without you. I've trained you to do everything for me," he said. "I love you. I love you very much."

But I had had enough of his idea of love. Love for Ivry was constant flattery and fetching things for him like a trained spaniel.

"Don't worry. You're always surrounded by beautiful young and old women. You won't be alone for long. And surely you'll be able to find some woman rich enough to buy you a Stradivarius violin, which an artist with your great talent deserves and you want so badly. I need a break. I feel old and burned out at twenty-five. I've never dated any man but you. I think you're a great violinist. I've had the privilege of helping your career in many ways. Just please understand I want some time to think over if I want to stay married to you for the rest of my life. I might someday want children, and I wouldn't want them to have a father who's cheating constantly on their mother. The thought of a little Ivry is too much for me. How could I ever take care of a child when you're the neediest, most spoiled child in the world? Besides, I want to find out who I am." Ivry couldn't imagine any woman dropping him. His conceitedness was as huge as his talent. "Look, we will stay in touch. A break would be good for both of us."

"Did Sidney put you up to this?" he asked, squinting his eyes.

Ivry always called my father by his first name. There was no love lost between the two of them. Behind his back, my father, who had a sense of humor, called his son-in-law "Gutless" instead of "Gitlis."

"No. This is all my idea, Ivry. Please understand. I've devoted myself to you for four years, really five years if you count our courtship, with all my energy and love. I want to be back in New York City for a while and start writing poetry again. Frankly, Ivry, don't be offended, but I'm tired of just being Madame Gitlis."

"There are plenty of women who would love to be Madame Gitlis," he said in that arrogant way that was pathetic because he wasn't joking.

"Find one, then."

"All right," he said in that voice of a grandiose maestro. A voice I had come to know so well. He started packing all his clothes into a battered suitcase that had stickers on it of all the countries we had toured. He then proudly picked up his violin and put it in the expensive alligator violin case which had been a gift to him from Jascha Heifetz, the great concert violinist who had befriended Ivry and admired his talent.

"Say goodbye to your generous father," he said sarcastically. "I'll send you a postcard from Vienna."

"We'll stay in touch," I said, trying to sound kind.

"Fuck you," Ivry said in French.

Then he slammed the door to my father's apartment and waited for the elevator, holding his violin case and his suitcase proudly. He was off to Vienna. I wouldn't be going with him. As the elevator descended, I screamed "Bravo."

3

Aunt Jewel and East End Avenue

"What happened last night?" my father's girlfriend, who I called Aunt Jewel, asked me. "You came home at nine in the morning. Before your daddy went to the office, he wanted to call the police. You know how neurotic he is about something happening to you."

"For God's sake, Aunt Jewel, I've been married for three years and lived in Europe. You should tell Daddy that sometimes I go to jazz clubs and stay up very late, until dawn."

There was no point inventing a story for Aunt Jewel. I had to be truthful. Aunt Jewel and I were best friends. She could tell if I was lying. She was a unique and amazing woman with the patience of a saint to put up with my difficult father for so many years. When I was twelve years old, a throw-away kid dumped for nine years in a boarding school, my Daddy was in the habit of driving up and visiting me every other Sunday with a different "aunt" sitting in his yellow Packard convertible with a hood ornament of a silver swan. On visiting days, my father would alternate Sundays with my mother and her husband Joe. Often neither of them would show up, and I would sit at a window waiting for them while everyone else went out with their parents. But when my father did come, I was so happy. To please my father, every new bimbo he arrived with in his Packard convertible had to be called "Aunt," but no woman lasted very long with my father. Back in those days he was handsome and amusing, and every woman thought he was a great catch. Every woman played up to him, hoping to "snag" a single millionaire. As soon as they found out that Sidney didn't ever want to get married again, that Sidney was cheap, and that the only person Sidney really could love was his only daughter, they gave up on him. Not Aunt Jewel. She didn't care if they were married or not. She really loved him. I had met her when I was eleven. She had driven up on a "Daddy Sunday" with my father, and had bought me a present. It was a black terra-cotta piggy bank with flowers on it. It came from Saks Fifth Avenue, where she worked. I remember loving the funny little piggy bank. Soon Aunt Jewel was driving up with my father without any competition. He had gone out with heiresses, movie stars, and models, but the true sweetness of Aunt Jewel had turned him into a faithful partner. Soon after they began dating, Aunt Jewel moved in with my father. I think one of the factors that endeared her to him was that she adored me, and I returned her love. She became my confidante, and I became very grateful to her for giving my father so much love.

As we sat on the couch in the living room, Jewel's life story floated through my mind. Aunt Jewel's story was unique. She had literally been found in a basket at a Catholic orphanage in Washington, D.C. in 1915. The young nun who discovered her gave her away to an elder sister who was Amish and lived in an Amish community. As a child, Jewel grew up in Pennsylvania, adhering strictly to the simple rules of the faith. When Aunt Jewel was thirteen, a tragedy happened: her adopted parents, riding in their horse and buggy, were run over by a hit-and-run driver and killed instantly. After that, Aunt Jewel was on her own. She told me that at thirteen she had looked older than she really was and went on the stage as a dancer in vaudeville. She later worked at Hicks, a specialty food and gift basket store off Madison Avenue frequented by the very rich. She met her first husband there, who she still referred to as "Mr. Bamberger." He was related to the Rothschilds. His family owned a large department store in New Jersey. But according to Jewel, he was spoiled and never worked a day in his life. I never learned his first name. This was just before World War II broke out. According to her story, Mr. Bamberger brought Aunt Jewel to Vienna to meet his widowed mother, a wealthy cousin of the Rothschilds. He thought she would never approve of a marriage to a poor Catholic shop girl. But, not surprisingly, Mr. Bamberger's aristocratic mother adored Aunt Jewel. Jewel and Mr. Bamberger were married in Vienna with his mother's blessings. The Duke and Duchess of Windsor and several other members of European royalty attended the small but elegant wedding. Since the wedding took place just before the war, Aunt Jewel was asked by her new Jewish mother-in-law to sneak some of the Rothschild jewels out of Europe in her girdle. She saved many of the Rothschilds' jewels and gave them to her husband to distribute. But she soon became bored with Mr. Bamberger. She left him one day without even asking for a penny or seeing him again. (She only saved her 500-year-old diamond ring and gave it with love to me, when I was married, as her gift. I always wear it on my left hand and think of her with love.) She then made a living by selling scarves at Saks Fifth Avenue. When she was in her early thirties, she met my father on a blind date. They never married, but Jewel soon became his constant female companion. Aunt Jewel adored my father.

She took care of him and lavished on him all of her love. I felt so happy for my father, who had been so hurt by my mother's leaving him and had been put through a heartbreaking custody case, which he never won. It relieved my feelings of guilt when I moved, at twenty-two, to live in Paris, that he had someone to take care of him. I loved my father so much. Aunt Jewel was truly a loving friend. She was upset when I arrived early in the morning still dressed in the clothes I had worn to work.

"I wasn't listening to jazz. I fell in love," I confessed to Aunt Jewel.

I was still filled with the euphoria of falling instantly in love with Cal.

"Good for you, sweetheart," Aunt Jewel said. "Who is the lucky man?" I was smiling for the first time in months with true joy. "Tell me."

"He's a great poet, Robert Lowell. Everyone calls him Cal. He's the king of American poets. Everyone who reads English and American literature looks up to him. I first met him when I was only a junior at Bennington in Cambridge. I attended his class, went back to Bennington, got married, and never thought about him again. But I did read his poetry, in Paris, constantly. Ivry often left me alone when he went on tour, and I sat in bed, memorizing Lowell's poetry and learning from the brilliance of his cadences and rhymes and odd connections. At that time, I adored him with the adoration of a young poet. I admired him for his authentic and magnificent body of work. Then, yesterday, he agreed to let me interview him for a magazine called *Encounter* at the Russian Tea Room. I told him I was married but separated from my husband, and he revealed that his own marriage was over and he was in the process of separation as well. He's now living in New York with his cousin. We both felt so attracted to each other that we wound up making love after a beautiful experience, a walk on the Brooklyn Bridge, when he read me a poem by Hart

Crane and told me he loved me. He wants to marry me. He even talked about us being buried together in his family plot in Dunbarton, New Hampshire, so we could be next to each other through eternity."

"The Brooklyn Bridge? Why there? Is he crazy?" Aunt Jewel asked. "And why would he want to talk about being buried together when he'd just met you?"

She was more than a little uncomfortable with my first adventure since I had gotten separated and moved to New York City. She seemed concerned.

"I think he wanted to impress on me his eternal love. Or perhaps he just didn't want to be under the earth with all the Winslows and Lowells without a woman he loves next to him. I understand how he feels," I said with all my young compassion and enthusiasm about suddenly falling in love.

Dear Aunt Jewel had never heard of Hart Crane or Robert Lowell. She was dumbfounded by this news. She didn't want me to be heartbroken by some older married man.

"Is he an opportunist like Ivry?" she asked.

"No. He's got plenty of money. He's a Lowell. After he read that beautiful and inspiring poem, he suddenly told me his secret. He wants to marry me. And you know what? I think I could be happy with him forever."

"Marry you? Where? On the Brooklyn Bridge? When? During rush hour? With all those cars?"

She laughed. She was making fun of me.

"Please don't laugh. It's happening. We fell in love."

"This man, whoever he is, sounds a little *meshuga*," Aunt Jewel said. Even though she was not Jewish, she had picked up a few Yiddish expressions from my father.

"In that case, we're both a little crazy," I said. "No poet is a normal person. And what is normal, anyway? People can fall in love instantly. 'Lunatics and lovers,' that was what Shakespeare wrote about in his comedies and tragedies. Instant love can happen, you know. Besides, you always told me you fell in love with Daddy at first sight."

"Well, that was different," Aunt Jewel said, willing to admit instant love was possible. "What is this poet like?"

"He's tall. Courteous. Beautiful eyes. Good-natured. He's built like a football player. He has a great sense of humor. He's been married twice, and he's left his current wife. That, by the way, he swears, has nothing to do with me. He told me he was backing out of his marriage long ago and had already signed the lease on an apartment before we met for lunch. He wants a divorce."

"Oh, please," Aunt Jewel said cynically. "That's what they all say. He could be lying."

She then began laughing at my naïveté and gullibility.

"It's true," I said, upset that she didn't even ask about our plans for our new life. "You'll see. He promised me we would be very happy."

"Darling girl," Aunt Jewel said, "You have led a sheltered life. First boarding school, then college, then a little acting, then marriage. You're still so innocent," Aunt Jewel remarked sadly. "He probably just wanted to sleep with a pretty, young, rich girl. I trust men as far as I can throw a Steinway piano."

She meant to be humorous. I was now annoyed.

"I'm not that pretty. And he has no idea that Daddy is rich. I'm going to get a divorce as soon as possible. It's all going to work out beautifully. You'll see." I added, "You'll be my maid of honor at our wedding."

Aunt Jewel looked dubious. She wanted to protect me from being hurt again. Ivry's cheating on me all during our marriage had warned her that I was too trusting. She had heard me crying myself to sleep. She was mistrustful of my judgment. She didn't want that heartbreak for me again. My marriage to a romantic concert violinist who lived the "high life" in Paris had certainly been a flop.

"I don't think your father is going to be happy about this. He was not thrilled with a violinist. Now a poet? Your father is hoping you will immediately divorce Ivry and marry a solid citizen—a lawyer, or a banker, or one of the sons of his wealthy friends who serve on the board of his hospital. A poet? At the very least he doesn't approve of your eccentric beatnik friends. Who was that man with a dark beard who sat on the living-room floor singing with a harmonica? Allen something? He wants you to move away from that nighttime beatnik crowd that you hang out with all the time in the West Village."

"Robert Lowell is not a beatnik, Aunt Jewel. His family arrived in America on the *Mayflower*. He's the ultimate WASP from an aristocratic Boston Brahmin family. He's a Lowell. He's a genius as far as I'm concerned. He's the greatest American poet of the twentieth century. You're going to meet him." I ran to my bedroom and brought out one of his books of poetry which I always kept on my desk, *Lord Weary's Castle*. I proudly showed Aunt Jewel the picture of the handsome man on the back of the dust jacket. I was passionately in love.

"He's good-looking," she said reluctantly. "But does he have any money? Most aristocrats I've met are totally broke phoneys."

"I have no idea, but I'm sure he makes a good salary teaching at Harvard and the New School, where he's teaching now. He also lectures at literary conferences all over the world."

The chance for Aunt Jewel to meet my new love came the next day. Cal called me early in the morning.

"Come and see it," he said into the phone.

"See what?"

"My new apartment," he said with excitement.

"You found one immediately?" I asked, amazed.

"Yes, my cousin knew a real estate broker who found the apartment, on East End Avenue. That's exactly where I want to live, as I told you, on the Upper East Side. I'm only a few blocks away from you."

"This is exciting," I said. "But first, please come over and meet my Aunt Jewel, my father's girlfriend. I want her to love you as I do," I whispered into the phone. "She's very important to me."

"If she's important to you, she's important to me," he said in a voice that told me he was as giddy with excitement as I now was. "I'm coming to pick you up in half an hour. 929 Park Avenue is about five blocks from my new bachelor pad. Even less." He hung up.

True to his word, in half an hour Cal was in the lobby of 929 Park Avenue. Our white-gloved doorman rang us on the intercom, and in one new moment of happiness, I threw open the door. We embraced. Cal stood in the doorway for a moment to take in the scene.

"What a beautiful apartment," he said. A Napolean-era mirror, gold sconces, and Impressionist paintings hung on the wall of the living room. The furniture was French provincial and covered in pastel silk.

"It's Aunt Jewel's taste," I said.

I introduced him to Aunt Jewel. He looked very handsome, very Episcopalian and classy. I could tell Aunt Jewel was pleasantly surprised that he wasn't wearing on his head a beanie with a propeller on it, like Allen Ginsberg had when he visited me at Daddy's apartment to read his poems to me. Cal explained that he had just rented his new apartment and was starting a new life. Aunt Jewel was a bit overwhelmed by this personal confession, but she was very warm and polite and offered Cal a Scotch on the rocks, which he accepted immediately. We both joined him in a drink, even though it was only four in the afternoon. I rarely drank, but had a sip of the Scotch so we could all clink glasses.

"I hope to see more of you," Cal said to Aunt Jewel as we were leaving.

I could tell she was now our advocate. I was glad Cal had impressed her. After we left my father's apartment, I asked Cal:

"What did you think of daddy's girlfriend?"

"She's a lovely woman," Cal said. "I can tell she loves you."

"She does," I said.

"I love you too," he said in a soft voice with such tenderness, I had tears in my eyes.

He held my hand and squeezed it. We walked, with our arms around each other's waists, to East End Avenue. When we arrived at 85 East End Avenue, Cal introduced me to the doorman of the building.

"Michael," he said, "this is my fiancée, Sandra. I'm a lucky guy."

"You certainly are," the young doorman of 85 East End Avenue said in a thick Irish accent.

"I'm giving her the key to my apartment," Cal told him. "And she can come and go as she likes, day or night, without being announced."

"Yes, Mr. Lowell," Michael said in his sing-song Irish voice.

I could tell Cal liked him because he looked a little bit like a younger version of President Kennedy, for whom Cal had voted so enthusiastically, he told me, in the presidential election. The doorman seemed to enjoy welcoming a new couple into the building. Cal had made me a set of his keys, and he gave them to me. Yes. We were a couple. A couple of crazy poets in love.

We kissed in the elevator as we rode to the fifteenth floor. Cal opened the door to his bachelor digs. He told me it was to be our "temporary home" until we were both divorced and got married, which he said with such assurance that I really was positive he meant what he said.

"And then what?" I asked, teasing him flirtatiously.

"And then I'll be your king and you'll be my queen," he answered as if singing the children's nursery rhyme that ended with "dilly dilly."

His new apartment was sparsely furnished. I noticed a small, black bust of Napoleon on his desk. It was sunny. The kitchen had a window looking out at the water. So did the large living room. Even the large bedroom and Cal's study looked out at the bright blue water of the East River. Tugboats that were painted red, white, and black were moving in slow motion up and down the East River. The view was perfect for Cal.

"I brought my things in a cab this morning," Cal said, proud of his dubious organizational talents. "I have everything I want."

"Why Napoleon?" I asked.

"That's what my mother called me when I was a little boy."

Surprisingly, his clothes were neatly hanging in a closet. We kissed each other and held each other for a long time. We were both experiencing new and poignant feelings of hope and desire.

The entrepreneurial young doorman, always looking for a generous tip, had given Cal access to a cleaning woman. She had helped him, he told me, arrange his books and clothes. The large closets held a few sports jackets, a dark hand-tailored suit, and several pairs of shoes, mostly moccasins because Cal confided "I don't like shoelaces." On the shelves, the maid had arranged his freshly laundered shirts and cashmere sweaters. Even the bathroom was set up with his Dunhill leather shaving kit, which had his initials RTL stamped in gold. *Very classy,* I thought. His bottle of Bay Rum cologne stood on the sink along with small bottles of eye fluid for contact lenses. It was as if some miraculous fairy godmother had made everything perfect. Most of all, Cal was proud of his study. He had his Olivetti typewriter set up with a stack of virgin white paper and had brought his white metal file cabinet. On top of his desk sat the small black bust.

"Hello, Mr. Bonaparte. I'm going to keep you company," I said with a laugh.

"Napoleon was smart and bossy. And so am I. But you'll get used to it, my darling."

He paused. What made me take a deep breath of amazement was when he pointed out that in the living room he had set up another desk, with a second Olivetti typewriter.

"Why two offices?" I asked.

"The other Olivetti typewriter is for you. I had two. This is where you can write your poetry." I took a deep breath. "We can write together," he said lovingly.

I felt a momentary rush of gratitude for Cal's acknowledgement of my writing. Cal was proud of all his arrangements. He was the Wizard of Oz and he was giving me a tour of his own Emerald City. With my own office on East End Avenue, I felt like Dorothy, who would never go back to Kansas or Park Avenue.

"Cal, I have a secret to tell you. I have been so inspired by falling in love with you that I began writing a new poem last night. It's called 'Ivory and Horn.' The idea for the poem began five years ago when I was living in Cambridge and sitting in on Professor Harry Levin's lectures at Harvard. According to Dr. Levin, the ancient Greeks believed there were two gates of sleep. One of ivory for true dreams, the other of black horn for false dreams. Last night I began this poem that is going to be about us. I imagined a change from the dark gates of sleep to the new gates of Ivory. I just have the first lines written."

I began reading "Ivory and Horn."

1
I am locked in the kitchen, let me out.
Burning in the toaster,
Sizzling in the pan,
Choked in the gas range,
Iced in the kitchen glass,
Broken in the bowl,
I jumped out of the cup.
Throw dishrags on my anger,

Crumbs over my head, anoint
Me for the marriage bed.
The bride is buttered, eaten when she's charred.
Her husband falls into a tub of lard.

2
Under a green comforter,
Waiting for love,
The heart of the city breaks
In my pillow, and down
The streets parade great cats
With wedding tails
And huge plumed hats.

"It's magnificent, but I really don't want to comment or rewrite anything just yet," Cal said. "Keep writing. The most important thing a poem can do is flow from the truth. So far the poem is fresh, vivid, and direct. The beginning is imaginary, and it has a skillful and memorable cadence in the odd beginning. Don't stop."

"I won't," I said. "I want 'Ivory and Horn' to be a collection of fears and myths, as well as moments of tenderness, regret, torments, sensuality, and the music of the unconscious."

Cal looked at me with such kindness in his eyes. He sighed as if he envied, for a moment, my youth.

"I admire your intensity," he said. And then he continued, wistfully: "Perhaps you can bring your youth and intensity into my life again. Right now I'm going through a dry period. I'm teaching at the New School and rewriting my book *Imitations* to keep myself busy. Would you mind some evening reading out loud my book, *Imitations,* and giving me your opinion?"

"Of course not." I said.

He then gave me a galley of *Imitations* held together with paper clips to study. He signed it for me. He wrote in his small black print, "for Sandra, the love of my life."

Suddenly we felt so close to each other that we kissed for a long time. Yes. He was right. We were living out the English folk song, "Roses are red/dilly dilly/roses are green/when you are king/dilly dilly/I'll be your queen." I had packed a small suitcase with some personal things to add to his apartment, such as a red velvet pillow for his bed. Also, a Swedish straw angel which I had bought for myself when I had traveled to Sweden the summer of my fifteenth year. I had traveled with the Academic Travel Association at the suggestion of Dr. Christina Van Holstein, the dean of my boarding school, who had convinced my father that travel "was the best education for a young person." I also bought two of my favorite books and placed them in the living room along with my gift of the pillow, and the gift of the small Swedish angel.

"I hope we will have many happy days here," Cal said after he thanked me for the presents.

"We will. These humble gifts are for good luck in your new home," I said.

Soon we were lying down on the huge king-size bed in Cal's bedroom. We lay in each other's arms. It was beautiful to make love and afterwards look out at the East River. Cal then got up to place a record of a symphony, by Aaron Copland, on the turntable of his new hi-fi set. We listened to the music in each other's arms. Then we took a shower together. Every moment was electric. We both felt so passionate about each other. I couldn't have imagined before how loving him would change everything. Every detail of his apartment took on a new significance just because he existed. Passion made every moment important. There is no realism like the insatiable realism of love. Suddenly I stood back and just observed him. When you desire someone so much and he's right there in front of you, there is something prayerful about not touching and just letting the light caress your bodies. It was a heavenly morning. As Cal kissed me, everything seemed so alive.

Everything seemed so animated. Everything in the bedroom seemed to speak to me of my passion. Everything, every new object invited me to cherish it. It was only the third time we had been together, but it was as if we had never lived without each other. He kept saying over and over, "You're beautiful."

The first thing we did in our new neighborhood was to take a walk along the East River. I looked up at all the buildings along the river that had little terraces on them. The private school for girls, Brearley, was right near the water walk. Several young girls in their school uniforms were playing hopscotch and singing. As we walked down the river's edge on a path lined with benches, I felt like singing too. We then sat on a bench, holding hands and staring like an old couple at the river. I felt rapture. The moment was so beautiful that we first sat in silence looking at the river.

"Which is your favorite poem of mine?" Cal asked. I could tell he was fishing for compliments from me, but I found that endearing.

"Oh, Cal. There are so many. How can I choose? I guess 'Skunk Hour.'"

"I have to tell you how I chose the title for my new book, *Imitations.* I was stuck for a title because all the poems are loose translations. In order to make them work as poetry in English with the right rhythms and cadences, I changed a lot of them, and I'm afraid they all sound Lowellesque a bit. A lot of critics such as Dudley Fitts were very angry at my taking such liberties, but I wrote to Randible—that's Randall Jarrell, who I must say will always be my best friend—and he wrote back, 'What do you care about his review? Dudley Fitts never wrote a line of poetry in his life.' He went on to say 'Fitts doesn't know what the hell he's talking about.' Randible loves them and so does Stanley Kunitz. I can't wait for you to meet Stanley Kunitz and his wife, who live right here in New York. I have so many poets that I love that I want you to meet them all. Randall

Jarell, Elizabeth Bishop, Allen Tate, John Crowe Ransom, T. S. Eliot, W. H. Auden, Sylvia Plath, Adrienne Cecile Rich, the list goes on and on."

"I'm planning to write my master's thesis at Columbia on Elizabeth Bishop. I love her poems. They changed my life," I said in a whisper.

"I can't believe it! She's one of my best friends and favorite poets. You have to meet her!" Cal said with delight and surprise that she, of all poets, would be the subject matter of my thesis.

He told me he and Elizabeth Bishop were each other's favorite "critics" and wrote letters to each other constantly.

"I live for those letters," he blurted out, and added, "I also help her get grants."

To me, this was all happening in a dream. I was a nobody, but Cal had access to everyone. Many of Cal's friends, T. S. Eliot, W. H. Auden, Randall Jarrell, Richard Wilbur, Elizabeth Bishop, were some of my favorite post–World War II poets, but I'd never imagined that I would meet any of them. I had studied their work and their lives and memorized many of their poems from the time I knew at Bennington that I was going to devote my life to poetry. Their poetry had been taught by Francis Golfing in my modern poetry class. That class was also where I discovered *Lord Weary's Castle*. There was a sincere Catholic devotion to God, as well as desperation, in *Lord Weary's Castle*. I never dared think that the brilliant poet who wrote that book would become the love of my life.

"Which of my poems do you like the best?" Cal asked again.

I answered, "How many hairs do I have on my head? I love all of them."

"But if you had to choose one?"

"I can't. There are too many that I memorized and keep inside me and refer to when I am alone. But I love the religious poems. I've often considered becoming Catholic," I said.

Cal was now surprised.

"But you're Jewish," he said in surprise.

"My two favorite women poets, St. Teresa of Avila and Simone Weil were Jews who converted to Catholicism. When I was in boarding school I wanted to be Catholic because the captain of the Cherry Lawn football team was Catholic, and I imagined I was in love with him. I'm not religious. I believe in God. My Irish Catholic nurse weaned me on the milk of Catholicism," I admitted. I went on: "I love 'Mr. Edwards and the Spider.' That's the poem that transports one into the world of John Edwards. I love the first part of 'Mother and Son' and 'Between the Porch and the Altar,' so many," I said.

I recited "Mr. Edwards and the Spider" out loud. Cal was surprised that I knew every word. He kept hugging me as we left the park bench and walked along the river's edge.

"What makes you write poetry?" Cal asked all of a sudden.

"Who can say? It's as if I have all these thoughts inside my head, like songs made out of jellyfish. They crawl down my shoulders from my brain and down the veins of my arm, melting into the tips of my fingers; then I write."

"Fire in your belly and ice in your fingers," Cal said, laughing. "I like that."

"How do you write?" I asked Cal shyly. "How do you begin your poems?"

"Oh, sweetheart, they begin with whatever I am thinking. Afterwards I add the rhymes. It's the cadences and rhymes that make it all better. They help to order what I'm trying to say."

I was shocked to find out that rhymes actually came as afterthoughts. As the weeks passed, every day I was learning something new about Robert Lowell's genius. After a few weeks of being together, he was busy revising my poetry and also giving me suggestions. They were magical corrections. One morning I summoned up the courage to read him the next part of "Ivory and Horn."

3
Underneath the city
There is this: paws of a tiger.
For I have seen true dreams
Are white nights lit by black neon lamps.
I have seen the stripes
Of True and Untrue dreams:
There are two gates of sleep; one of Horn
For true visions,
The other, shining, of white Ivory,
Through which ghosts
Send false dreams.

The bridegroom by himself is slain. Ivory
To Horn is chained.

4
I saw a kitten with a tiger's head
Chewing up nine lives. Dead
Sperm lice clinging to his catty snout,
He crawled back to the bag that let him out.
"When you find the Tiger, kill him!" they said.
I could not sleep. I walked about
New York and looked for him.
In the daytime on the park's green lip I stood.
Blood in my mouth flowing like a stream of angry water.
Armed, at night, I ferried the East River,
And pounded on his door. The doorman came,
A blue lion tamer shooing off his game.

Soon, with his black fountain pen, he crossed out a few of my words and added a few of his own on my poem. I began to wonder now, is it sex or poetry that keeps us together? We were writing and rewriting poems, but it was the beauty of an almost religious love that was in my new life with Cal.

"I want you to know this," Cal said. "Even though I have only known you for a few weeks, I am never away from you. You are always in my mind. I shall never leave you. In another world I shall still be the one who loves you, loves you beyond measure. You have given me what I always wanted: a new life without arguments, without tears. Your face lights up when you see me, as if someone has turned on a light switch. I cannot love you enough or ever show you my gratitude."

I hugged him. He knew I felt the same way. I wanted him to take me to church. Even though he was no longer a fanatical Catholic—he was, as he explained, lapsed—I wanted the experience of being in a Catholic church with him. We went to a 7:30 mass one Sunday night at the Church of St. Ignatius Loyola at 980 Park Avenue. We listened to the choir and chamber orchestra. The priest in his green and gold robe gave a sermon on love, reading from a portion of the hymnal. It was letters from I Corinthians that had been read over and over in my boarding school's morning meetings, where we began our day, after breakfast, with the entire upper and lower school sitting on the outdoor assembly porch, listening to one of the students read. Everyone had to take turns reading out loud whatever spiritual reading they picked. Many recitals were from the *Bhagavad Gita, The Wisdom of Confucius, The Book of the Dead, The Prophet, The Talmud, Mary Baker Eddy, The New Testament, The King James Bible, Native American Chance, The Talmud, I Corinthians.* Cherry Lawn, my boarding school alma mater, was a wildly progressive school in the hills of Connecticut where fresh air, art, and eclectic tastes for spirituality were encouraged. I also chose to read Native American chants or from the Talmud when I was in the lower school, but I loved I Corinthians. Cal recited the memorial acclamation response by heart.

"When we eat this bread, when we drink this cup, we proclaim your death, Lord Jesus, until you come, until you come in glory."

Cal knelt on the kneeler and so did I. We clasped our hands in prayer during the *Agnus Dei*. We stood together and sang hymns, including Cal's favorite hymns, "Blest Are They" and "I Come with Joy." The huge organ, which Cal told me was the largest organ in any church in New York, chimed its divine pipes of music. I, a young Jewish woman, stared at the altar decorated with white sculptures and a huge likeness of Christ. The ceiling was magnificent, and as the congregation marched slowly to accept the wine and wafer from the priest and a female reader, I sat quietly in my seat. I wasn't Catholic, and I didn't want to pretend to be, but Cal took the wafer, swallowed it, drank wine from the cup, and returned to where we were sitting in the third row. During the concluding rites I felt that my parents, even though they were not religious (my mother went to a reform temple in Scarsdale every Friday and my father belonged to dozens of Jewish organizations) would pass out cold if they knew I was kneeling in a Catholic Church with my new boyfriend. But I didn't care what anyone thought of what I did. I had loved the Old Testament and the Talmud, but now I loved being at St. Ignatius Loyola mass with Cal. I lifted my voice and sang with joy. As Cal and I were leaving St. Ignatius Loyola Church, we both took a taper and lit candles. We each made our private prayers. I prayed for our love to last. I whispered my prayer into Cal's ear just before he put a dollar bill in the black offering box.

4

Visiting Scarsdale

In the weeks that were to come, we agreed that this was the most beautiful spring of our lives. The time that we spent together was going by quickly and was proving to be days of joy and awe. Cal also doted on the fact that I enjoyed housework.

"It's good therapy," I told him. "I love order. I like everything clean. I even love washing dishes."

"In this apartment we can eat on the floor," he said. "And you cover up the fact that I'm a slob. You're also getting me to stop drinking so much. Sometimes I think you're saving my life. Neither of my two wives was at all domestic," he told me.

"Too bad," I said, "for them."

I loved cooking, ironing, and cleaning. In our new life, Cal saw that I loved being his homemaker. He enjoyed it when I waxed the floor, dancing on rags, a technique I had picked up in Paris to clean floors and polish the wood so that our floors shone like mirrors. Cal, as he had admitted to me, was a messy person, always dropping his clothes on the floor, messing up his sweaters and shirts, but I didn't mind going to the cleaners or constantly picking up and doing laundry and ironing so he always looked neat. Cal was definitely a Calaban, a savage that I was trying to tame. He told me he loved my looking after him.

One day I came up with the idea that—since we were always talking about marriage—Cal should finally meet my mother and stepfather, Joe Barnett, who lived in Scarsdale. Cal liked this idea. At twenty-five, I was now happy that my mother was married to Joe, who I once had hated as a child; but in my twenties, I had grown to appreciate him as a fabulous step-father. I now truly loved him and forgave him for the past. My mother's husband had interests and hobbies that he shared with her, and she and Joe Barnett were almost always compatible. Joe Barnett had been a bandleader and musician at Syracuse University, where he went to law school. He and my mother both loved Classical music. Tchaikovsky, Beethoven, and Stravinsky played often on his precious stereo that no one but he was allowed to touch. He was also an amateur magician and a lawyer who represented many great magicians pro bono. Joe, in fact, was the founder of the New York City Magician's Roundtable that met every weekday for lunch at the Edison Hotel. There, all the professional magicians came to meet, lunch, and swap tricks. Only magicians were allowed to attend this roundtable. With Joe and my mother, I had attended dozens of magician's conventions and was always amazed when Joe did magic tricks. I especially loved his "lemon trick" where he held a lemon in one hand and a dollar in the other and then somehow made the dollar come out of the lemon by cutting the lemon in half. It was a remarkable sleight-of-hand miracle. Joe was a fabulous magician. He had been learning tricks from great magicians all his adult life. Whenever a magician needed a lawyer, they sought out Joe Barnett. He once told me they paid him in tricks.

My stepfather was also an avid fly fisherman, and I knew from Cal's beautiful poem about fishing for God that Cal was a fly fisherman also. I was sure he and Joe Barnett would get along. And so off we went by train from Grand Central one beautiful Saturday afternoon to my mother's home in Scarsdale. A cab took us to my mother's beautiful house. Joe Barnett was waiting at the door and warmly embraced us both. He led us into their warm and friendly home. Mom and Joe collected antiques. My mother asked Cal if he had ever read the novelist James Joyce. That was her favorite writer.

"Of course," Cal answered. "I even assigned *A Portrait of the Artist as a Young Man* to my creative writing class at the New School."

My mother was impressed. I could tell that, like Aunt Jewel, my mother thought Cal to be very charming and polite. He had even bought a bottle of expensive wine at Grand Central as a gift. I had told my mother that Cal was brilliant and that he had not only won the Pulitzer Prize but had studied all the classics and even knew Greek. But I think it impressed my mother that he also had read her favorite writer. We clinked glasses.

"Call me Mae," my mother said.

Cal looked at a framed picture of my mother in a cap and gown taken when she had received her master's degree in education from Columbia.

"My God, you were so beautiful. Now I know where your daughter gets her good looks," he said.

I saw to my surprise that my mother was blushing. That afternoon we all sat down in the dining room and ate Chinese food that Joe, also a master chef, had cooked for this special occasion. Cal refused, politely, to use chopsticks, but I always ate Chinese food with chopsticks, and Cal was envious of my dexterity. Mom's dining room looked out through huge glass windows onto a patio and beyond that to her and Joe's beautiful rose garden. My mother, who was not only a schoolteacher but a literary person, reacted well to the fact that I was now in love with a great poet even if he was much older than I was. The news that as soon as we both were divorced we were planning to marry seemed to please her. A true genius was coming into the family after all. My mother had made a pilgrimage to the Scarsdale bookstore and bought Cal's books of poetry. She had spent weeks reading *Lord Weary's Castle, Mills of the Kavanaughs,* and *Life Studies* and loved Cal's talent. He signed the books for her. She told Cal his poetry was historic and that her favorite poem was "For the Union Dead." She asked Cal how he had come to write that particular poem, and Cal explained, very modestly, that he had been commissioned to write it. Then effortlessly, the conversation happily turned to fly-fishing. I begged Cal to recite for my mother and stepfather "The Drunken Fisherman," his famous religious fishing poem. I thought he would refuse, but to my surprise, he stood up in front of the big bay window and recited the poem as if he was giving a reading at a university:

> Wallowing in this bloody sty,
> I cast for fish that pleased my eye
> (Truly Jehovah's bow suspends
> No pots of gold to weight its ends);
> Only the blood-mouthed rainbow trout
> Rose to my bait. They flopped about
> My canvas creel until the moth
> Corrupted its unstable cloth.
>
> A calendar to tell the day;
> A handkerchief to wave away
> The gnats; a couch unstuffed with storm
> Pouching a bottle in one arm;
> A whiskey bottle full of worms;
> And bedroom slacks: are these fit terms

To mete the worm whose molten rage
Boils in the belly of old age?
Once fishing was a rabbit's foot—
O wind blow cold, O wind blow hot,
Let suns stay in or suns step out:
Life danced a jig on the sperm-whale's spout—
The fisher's fluent and obscene
Catches kept his conscience clean.
Children, the raging memory drools
Over the glory of past pools.

Now the hot river, ebbing, hauls
Its bloody waters into holes;
A grain of sand inside my shoe
Mimics the moon that might undo
Man and Creation too; remorse,
Stinking, has puddled up its source;
Here tantrums thrash to a whale's rage.
This is the pot-hole of old age.

Is there no way to cast my hook
Out of this dynamited brook?
The Fisher's sons must cast about
When shallow waters peter out.
I will catch Christ with a greased worm,
And when the Prince of Darkness stalks
My bloodstream to its Stygian term . . .
On water the Man-Fisher walks.

When Cal was reciting we had all been enthralled. After he
finished we were silent. I wondered if my mother realized how
rare it was for Cal to recite his poetry for people that he didn't
know really well. My mother and Joe thanked Cal profusely
for this spontaneous recitation.

"What exactly is confessional poetry?" my mother asked as she helped herself to another thick crystal goblet of the red wine Cal had bought.

My stepfather Joe rarely drank, but he dusted off his secret bottle of old and expensive Scotch on this special occasion. Though he didn't think Scotch went as well as tea with Chinese food, we all had Scotch with our meal. Meeting for the first time as a "family" was a great moment for all of us. One of America's most celebrated writers was spending the day with my mom and stepfather. Mom made a toast:

"To the first confessional poet in our family."

"I don't really like being called a Confessional Poet," Cal said sweetly to my mother. "I just translated Racine's *Phaedra*, and God knows not all of my poetry comes out of my own experience. M. L. Rosenthal, the critic, called Allen Ginsberg's book *Kaddish* confessional. But I don't like that word. However, because of my book *Life Studies,* I seem to be lumped in the same confession box. I told the poet, Fred Seidel, one of my favorite young poets, in the interview that he wrote about me in the *Paris Review,* that the realist poet serves an accuracy that is not the accuracy of fact. Almost the whole problem of writing poetry, I told Fred, is to get back to what you really feel. That takes maneuvering. For example, in one of my so-called confessional poems 'To Speak of the Woe That Is in Marriage,' the wife puts ten dollars in her thigh." He smiled sheepishly. "But my wife never did that. I was told that story by the ex-wife of Delmore Schwartz and thought it was interesting so I added it to my poem. I think what I offer the reader is an invented world dense with the luminous opacity of life."

I know that Cal often invented truth, and I knew that many confessions were made up, but we all were feeling very honored to be able to ask him literary questions. My mother and Joe Barnett were now interested in everything that Cal said. We moved from the dining table to the den, where Joe entertained us all with some of his mind-reading tricks,

He said to Cal, "Think of a number from one to a hundred." And he then guessed right.

"Amazing!" Cal said.

He couldn't believe Joe's magical perfect guess. Joe then performed his lemon trick as the finale. Cal was the straight man for the lemon trick. Cal loved being the dummy. He loved it all. He was having a great afternoon. I felt so grateful to Joe Barnett for being so gracious and entertaining as well. We were all going to be a family. My mother applauded Cal after he was the straight man for Joe's lemon trick. Then she said:

"What a wonderful education for my daughter—being with you, Cal. She wants to be a poet, you know."

"She *is* a poet," Cal said, correcting her, looking at me lovingly. "I'm her new professor." He smiled. "She's writing a great poem called 'Ivory and Horn,' and I'm helping her. In fact, she writes poetry all the time."

Joe's huge dog, a smelly brown and white English Setter named Duke, entered the room and banged his tail with love against the floor. Cal and Duke took to each other. We were all laughing and drinking. I was secretly thrilled that Cal, my mom, and my stepfather were getting along so well. Joe was telling Cal before long how he became a fly-fisherman as a boy. He made his own flies. He took out his plastic box filled with hooks and threads. He told Cal where he bought the threads to make his own flies. Cal was impressed with the art of fly-making and marveled as Joe demonstrated how he created flies for fishing. They talked about fly-fishing for about an hour while Mom and I just listened. Without my knowing why, the conversation turned to marriage:

"Do you really have marriage intentions toward Sandra?" my mother asked in her most charming way of finding out the lay of the land without seeming obvious or too curious.

"Of course I do. I plan to have more children and be with her for the rest of my life," Cal answered, downing his whiskey and putting his arms around my mother, who he now called affectionately, Mae.

"But aren't you still married?" my mother asked tentatively, still very charming.

"I am. So is she. We both plan to divorce immediately." That was meant to end the conversation. But it only opened it up.

"Sandra has endured a very bad experience with Ivry. Now we realize that we should have stopped her when she was just twenty and ran off with him to Greece and later Israel before knowing he was a womanizer and an egomaniac. Also, Ivry thought Sandra came from a rich family. True, her father is comfortable, but Ivry thought he was marrying into enormous wealth. Sandra wasn't Doris Duke, and Ivry certainly never received a dime from Sidney. As it turned out, after they were married, they both lived in Paris on his income from concerts in Europe and some recordings, and he had very few of those. Unfortunately Sandy, as an American, legally couldn't get a job in Paris without having a green card. Ivry was furious that Sidney refused to support them. But, do *you* have the finances to support your ex-wife, a child, a new wife, and possibly more children?"

My mother was able to be curious and ladylike at the same time, sharing what was on her mind as a mother. I was a little mortified by my mother's frankness. Cal never talked about money. I had no idea what his financial situation was, and Aunt Jewel had told me "Gentiles don't like to talk about money," so I never brought up the subject. Cal laughed and found my mother's question endearing.

"Can I afford to get married again? I can. I live on a trust fund left to me by my grandmother. My parents are both dead; but I also do very well in my teaching. I must admit that as a Pulitzer Prize poet, I'm paid much more than I'm worth."

Spoken like a Lowell, I thought. When it was time to leave, my mother gave Cal a doggy bag filled with the rest of Joe's Chinese food that Cal had liked so much. What a day! I was overjoyed that now Cal had two fans in the Barnetts. It had been a unique day in Scarsdale history: poetry, feeding Chinese food to a literary celebrity, talk about marriage, and a few magic tricks, as well as a conversation about fly-fishing. Cal had gotten through the Jewish Hades of Scarsdale like Orpheus ascending.

On the train back to the city, I said, "You did brilliantly. I think both my mom and Joe fell in love with you."

"Now I want to meet your father. I can tell from your poems he's a real character," Cal said suddenly.

Oh, my God, that will be a disaster, a meeting from hell, I thought to myself. I dreaded the day. My father was not the charmer Joe Barnett was. The only things he liked to read were contracts or big numbers on dollar bills. I wasn't even sure he *could* read, as his secretary and Aunt Jewel were always reading to him or typing his letters. I was putting off the day of the big meeting and changed the subject. I didn't want to ever leave Cal; and I also protected him, since I loved him so much, from any of the alligators that opened their jaws and snapped at what was forbidden. I was still married. Cal was still married. Even though we were both plotting to divorce as quickly as possible, I knew that my father would think Cal was too old, too gentile, and too artsy for his beloved daughter. Even though I never listened to any advice my daddy gave me and was deaf to his complaints, Jewish *geshrys*, and *oy-vays*, still, I loved him, and didn't want to ever hurt him. I prayed to the Lord to put off the day of interaction between Sidney Pace Hochman and Robert Trail Lowell.

5

Grove Press Memories

After our first three months of bliss, Cal and I began to realize that we really were in love. We sat for hours getting to know each other, telling literary stories, talking about what had been important to us.

"What was the best time of your life?" Cal asked.

"In my senior year at Bennington College, in 1957, when I was lucky enough to get a job working for Barney Rosset at Grove Press. I was ecstatic. I was the assistant to Fred Jordan, who was a business manager for the exciting new magazine the *Evergreen Review,* edited by Barney Rosset and just being published for the first time. It was the first counterculture magazine that influenced hundreds of thousands of young writers. Barney, as everyone called him, was a most unusual man. As the publisher of a new company—which his ex-wife, the abstract expressionist painter, Joan Mitchell, helped him found—Barney was truly interested in publishing exciting, great literature. He was a bombshell in the literary world, brilliant, innovative, and someone who actually loved literature, as opposed to many of the other publishers who mostly saw publishing as a business. They were old-fashioned, while Grove Press was fresh and new. Almost all their books were published in paperback form and were inexpensive. They all had exciting, hip graphic designs on the covers. Barney had grown up in Chicago in a progressive school (similar to my own progressive school), and he was ready to take risks. He made literary history by challenging the authorities about publishing the original, uncensored version of D. H. Lawrence's *Lady Chatterley's Lover.* He won the legal battle and everyone was soon talking about Barney Rosset. (A few years later, he won the battle to print the controversial novel by Henry Miller, *Tropic of Cancer.*) Grove Press was very avant garde and had a small office in the Village. It soon became the center of New York's literary world. Barney surrounded himself with brilliant consultants, such as Don Allen, who really discovered the Beats. Don discovered Allen Ginsberg and Jack Kerouac, neither of whom was famous in 1957. The *Evergreen Review* was the first magazine to publish them. One day, Don Allen came into the office with these two grubby-looking writers. They were Allen Ginsberg and Jack Kerouac. Allen Ginsberg immediately began talking to me and asked me if I wrote poetry, and I shyly told him I did. Allen told me he would like to hear my work one day. He wore black glasses, and I thought he was very attractive in a charismatic way. Jack Kerouac was also very mellow and good-looking. He was wearing an old, brown, beat-up leather jacket. Unlike Ginsberg, he was quiet and shy. Ginsberg was very animated, while Kerouac looked uncomfortable. They seemed to like me, and Fred Jordan asked me to join Don, Jack, and Allen for lunch as his guest. I foolishly declined this lovely invitation because, frankly, I was shy and didn't want to impose myself on this all-male luncheon. I was always sorry that I didn't join them.

"One of Barney Rosset's greatest contributions was his discovering so many great authors, such as Samuel Beckett, Jean Genet, Tom Stoppard, William S. Burroughs, and Lawrence Ferlinghetti. Barney had been reading *Waiting for Godot* in a small French publication, and he asked my Bennington professor, Wallace Fowlie, who he used as a consultant, what he thought of it. Apparently Wallace Fowlie loved it and said that its nihilism would change world literature. As we know now, his prediction came true. Barney proceeded to publish all the works of Beckett. At night I would go home and read the paperback books of Beckett, the novels *Murphy* and *Molloy,* before anyone I knew had even heard of Beckett.

"At Grove Press I also met the Irish poet George Reavey, and, miracle of miracles, he invited me to a bar to meet Samuel Beckett and have a few beers with them. There I was, a nineteen-year-old girl, in love with literature, talking with one of the world's most original writers. I knew from Fred Jordan that Beckett, when he was younger, had been the secretary to James Joyce, and that really impressed me, as Joyce was, and still is, one of my favorite writers. Beckett was so brilliant. I was in awe of him. He was an Irish writer in the tradition of the Irish writers Yeats, O'Casey, Synge, George Bernard Shaw, and along with Joyce, the greatest of them all. I remember Beckett had a very thin face, and high cheekbones, crew-cut hair, and haunting huge eyes. As he stared at me, I blushed.

"The atmosphere at Grove Press was always exciting. You never knew which writer was going to come that day. Everyone knew Barney Rosset was an innovator. Grove Press not only brought experimental European literature into the mainstream, but it also caused an explosion of new American literature that was very political. Books and drawings change the world, and Barney's incredible taste in both helped foster the change. That's when I was the happiest in my life, Cal, when I was in that atmosphere. Barney always treated me like a young writer, not an employee."

Cal answered, "I had a similar epiphany at Kenyon College. John Crowe Ransom was publishing one of the most exciting intellectual magazines, the *Kenyon Review,* quite different than the *Evergreen Review,* and that is where I published my first poems. I was never happier than I was at Kenyon, so I understand why you were so happy working at Grove Press, being around innovators and great editors who had a talent for discovering art. It was a privilege that both of us shared, in our own different times, in the birth of two magazines that made the two greatest contributions to post–World War II poetry."

We were now divinely aware of our luck to have found each other, two romantic poets, madly in love, looking constantly into the mirrors of each other's eyes and never growing tired of making love or talking. I told Cal we were each other's newly discovered angels.

6

Lunch with Nancy Tish

What's it like to fuck a genius?" Nancy asked. She was a Bennington busybody, but I liked her.

"You see, Nancy, ever since I was a child I wanted someone to notice me for who I really am, and Robert Lowell is so appreciative of me and my poetry that I can't help but love him. When I read my poems out loud to him, I feel he understands me. Yes, the sex is great. It's great because the penis is partly shaped by a man's mind. The greater the mind, the greater the penis."

That shut her up. But only for a minute.

"What about identity?" Nancy surprised me by asking as she ordered another glass of wine. "Do you want to be known as Mrs. Lowell? You didn't appreciate being Madame Gitlis. Cal is almost twenty years older than you. He'll always be very famous. More than you are. You'll be in his shadow forever."

"My identity is my soul," I said spontaneously. "As far as I understand it, everyone has a soul that is unique, never to be replicated in the universe. I'll always keep my pen name, which is my maiden name. I don't have to be Mrs. Lowell. I can stay me."

"Well, don't become his satellite. And don't forget, keep telling him how great he is," Nancy said wisely. "You know the greatest gift a young girl can give an older man?"

"No."

"Her youth. And remember, all men love flattery," Nancy said as an expert on men.

She had a slight moustache, red hair, and before it was chic, space between her two front teeth. She had attitude also. Nancy was smart and talented. But there was something cynical about her tone of voice. I felt her jealousy. But who wouldn't be jealous? I was happy. I was young. And I was going to marry the world's most handsome and exciting poet. She couldn't top that with a banker.

"I don't have to flatter Robert Lowell," I said. "He's the most secure man I've ever met. I'm the one who feels insecure."

"Hey, babe, where's your self-esteem? The fact that you're cultured, you're a poet in your own right means he will stay interested. So don't be so insecure. Remember that really waspy girl at college? Deborah Cabot? She used to sing 'Boston has its beans, Boston has its cod, where the Cabots only talk to the Lowells and the Lowells talk only to God.' Poor Cal. He had to grow up in that world, hearing that song all his young life, especially at the snotty St. Marks School. He must have cringed every time someone spit that song in his face and tormented him about being a 'Lowell.' No wonder he wanted to change his life. You have to invite me to dinner one night," Nancy said, raising her hand for the waiter so she could order some more wine.

I was wondering if she should drink so much. It was too easy to become an alcoholic. One of the things I had helped

Cal with was to cut down on his drinking. I felt I really loved him and needed to take care of him. Who can tell us how to lead our lives? A line from my own poem ran through my brain like a mantra. I knew Nancy was trying to steal my happiness, like a thief. But she had no chance. What I had was really all to do with the spirit. And besides being a great lover, Cal was a spiritual man. I knew he loved me. And he loved the fact that I was a poet. I had written a new poem for him. I was going to show it to Nancy, but I changed my mind at the last minute. So I just sat there saying the poem over and over to myself in my head. I knew I would read it to Cal later.

Weary Love Poems

1
The attraction: the pull
Of rope—tying me to dark eyes, eyes
Of lumber, and the mouth
Is ripe. How do I praise
The maker? In a building
Made of glass—under the track-lights
And the ordinary ceiling
A dark man is thinking, feeling—
Caught—in the rapture of what?
The agent of all things is this:
The desire to make love. To take
Legs, and arms, and arteries
And blood—and more than that blood
Flowing: a sigh—the breath—
And make it all
The poem defeating death.

2
Or are you? Are you defeating
Death or merely flesh? Flesh the mother

And father—flesh the energy
And flesh the undresser. I remember reading in childhood about
The immaculate King of Thule
Who ran away from his women and his tower
To set sail—one night—alone into
The sea. Weary of power. Not
You: you drink
The image in and feel the rope
Of everything that is possible. Unknown
People in unknown dreams—unknown
Poems of unknown images—unsaid
Words on unknown paper—words
Go from poem to the skin. The poem is this:
A way of extending yourself into everyone,
To sit back, for example, in a bathtub
And have your poetry read in Barcelona, Peru, Santo Domingo,
Freeport, Normandy, to flash the image: SLEEP.

3
I see you. I sense you. Not as the
Maker despised by those poets and critics out of power—
Not as the hero of a thousand "meetings"
Where telephones are powerful as death,
But as the dreamer, the small boy
Inside that never got enough—
Of touch, of kisses, of thighs, of
Wonder, of things
That move and take you far away: airplanes
Swifter than the stream of blood,
Cars and the dark glasses of wine. Every day
A poem is made. Every day someone drops down
And the poetry flashes its own
Message: Awake awake. Forget the form,
That mistress with big tits larger than a goddess

And good enough to suck: the poetry world
Where business and teeth and power and lips
And aromas and sights take flight with the insane.

4
Some people are created to make
Mole hills. Or glaciers.You are
Not a mountain-climber—but a man
Who writes about the mountain. Can
Power be merely the flesh
That arms us for the battle: life or death?
Those who malign you
Secretly wish your wisdom: you, the
Quiet one—blessed
With your anger and pain. You want nothing
And encompass everything. Nothing holds you
Longer than perfection: you seek it
And you want nothing except All.You want the All.
All that you make is All.That is why
I trust you, I find your eyes
A word
For everything: I see in your eyes
A known quantity: Energy.
And more than that—deep feeling—
The feeling one has when one
Wants nothings—driven
Like a wild animal
To forget the lazy world of
Clocks and possibilities—the armed
Hero out to create—
A poem, but comes back
With colors, words, faces, the excitement
Of a city—comes home with pelts, history, confessions
Of flesh and power—and it is for this

That I lay under your arm
Breathing your smell into me. It was the smell
Of lumber, smell of hemp, smell of poetry
When it flaps against the
Old fashioned film editing machine
That slices the film
And then slices it again. No one
Wants more than you. No one seeks
Less power. You—who have
Covered yourself in words and have thrown your
Name across the pages of Europe, South America,
I see you. I see
The strong boy. The proud poet
That never got out.

7

Conversations at 85 East End Avenue

At dinner, Cal and I often read our poems out loud to each other. My book *Voyage Home* was being marked up by Cal. He revised all my poems with such relish that it moved me to tears to see the interest he took in my writing. I was so grateful to be learning from him. I so much admired the confessional poetry of his former students Sylvia Plath, Anne Sexton, and Adrienne Cecile Rich, all women poets who Cal not only encouraged but helped to elevate their careers in 1961. Poetry was still a man's world, and amongst other heroic things that Cal did was that he encouraged people to take women's writing seriously and campaigned for their publication. Without a doubt he was a male feminist of his time. His language was unique. He was rewriting my poems. His small black print from a fountain pen was carefully put over each line of

71

mine. I loved almost all of his suggestions. We sat on the couch in his study, looking at the lights blinking across the river.

"Should I read 'Freedom'?" I asked.

"Yes."

I picked up *Voyage Home* and read the poem:

I have grown tired of the water tap,
The bowing maids, the telephone messages, the crap.
From now on I will praise the water
That flows down me and to me and from me.
Marl, turf, red sod and barbed root, the dust
Are mint and sacrament.
Here is the household of the apple grass
Above the shut eye caverns of the worm
And I know both these kingdoms of the earth.
I also know the moon. One snowy-owl
Jogs down from Canada, wing over frozen cloud.
One snowy-wolf confronts me with his open jaw
As I devour seed
Of dandelion from Queen Anne's table weed.
Surely the Khan of Tartary once dwelt
Beneath a tent of felt. O tent of felt!

Cal smiled. "That's one of my favorite poems of yours because I like your Khan of Tartary. I once dwelt beneath a tent of felt myself, to get away from my parents," he said.

"You did? Tell me about it." I loved when Cal shared stories with me from his own life.

He identified with "Freedom" because it was about breaking away from the materialism of one's own family.

"I ran away from my family and from Harvard to a summer writing seminar in the South. There I met Allen Tate and John Crow Ransom, who became my great teachers. They were the poets and critics who inspired me at the writers' workshop I attended. When Ransom decided to leave the college he was teaching at in the South to go teach at Kenyon in Ohio, I left Harvard, after one year of being bored and learning nothing, to follow him. The summer before Kenyon, Ransom told me he had guests living with him, but I was welcome to join them. The guests turned out to be the great writer Ford Madox Ford and his wife, who I had met through Merrill Moore. Naturally I wanted to go."

"Oh, my God, Cal. Ford Madox Ford was one of my favorite novelists at Bennington. I wrote a paper on his novel *The Good Soldier*. You actually knew him?"

"Yes, I knew him. And he couldn't stand me. The Ransoms were generous enough to say I could live in a tent on their lawn until college began. I bought a tent, pitched it, and I was in literary heaven. But Ford constantly complained about me. He was a real prima donna. There wasn't enough water for bathing in the house and he blamed it on me being an extra person who used up the water. I was very messy in those days, and I think I never changed my clothes more than once all summer. He kept telling Professor Ransom, who loved me like a son, what a slob I was and that I smelled. He told Ransom that he was hoping they would get rid of me. But they never did, and Ford was furious that I remained in my tent. That summer that I lived in a tent on the Ransom property was the happiest summer of my life. I was just finding myself as a poet, and I could feel that constant excitement inside me when I wrote poems and showed them to Ransom. I was determined to follow John Crowe Ransom wherever he went. Later I changed my mind about Ford, but that summer he was definitely my enemy. I paid no attention to his complaints."

"And then what happened?"

"Then against my mother's and father's wishes, I went to Kenyon. My psychiatrist in Boston, Merrill Moore, who was also a poet, convinced my parents that I should go. You could imagine that Charlotte Winslow and Robert Trail Spence Lowell Sr. were very against it, but I was finally allowed to go, with Merrill Moore handling all the money details. That was the greatest time of my life. John Crowe Ransom changed Kenyon from a backwater small school for rich boys into a first-class literary college by founding the *Kenyon Review,* which is still the best literary magazine in America. And then I roomed in a small house with a group of boys who are still my close friends. There was Robie Macauley, Allen Tate, and Randall Jarrell and a few others, and we all wanted to be writers. We formed a special club, and it was a glorious time for all of just being separated from the all the other boys at the college and being eggheads and following our own creative writing."

"And then what?" I asked.

I moved closer to him on the couch and hugged him as he talked.

"And then I met Jean Stafford, my first wife. She had attended one of those writing conferences, and I found her to be very beautiful, very sophisticated. I admired the fact that she was a devoted convert to Catholicism. She was, I thought, also a very good short-story writer. I was bowled over by her intelligence and sophistication. She came from out West, and the first thing she did when she had gotten her hands on some money was to go to Europe and study in Germany. I was impressed with her European sophistication.

"Jean was well-read and smart. I loved that. She was Catholic; and while I was living with her, after we were married, I converted to Catholicism and became a Catholic fanatic. I went to live with Trappist monks; I stood on soap-boxes and tried to convert people to Catholicism. You cannot imagine that I finally had found my mission in life, and I was filled with fervor. I immersed myself in the rhythms of Gerard Manley Hopkins, whose poems came from the heart of a Jesuit. Jean and I were living in Louisiana then, where I was teaching at the University of Louisiana, in steaming, verminous heat. We sent away for Cardinal Newman's works, and as soon as they arrived, the cockroaches the size of larks relished the seasonal glue of the bindings and began eating the books by night. My Catholic instructor at Louisiana State University where I was teaching had chosen Baton Rouge, Louisiana as his parish because it gave him such an excellent chance to chasten his flesh. I had a good friend called Patrick Quinn, who was an ardent Catholic. He became the sponsor for my baptism into the Roman Catholic Church. I'm afraid that I became a round-the-clock obsessive. In the spring of 1941, Jean worked at a publisher and brought home all these Catholic books from the publisher, Sheed and Ward. I read every one of them. I was more Catholic than the Pope. I was determined to be monogamous with Jean until death. I know my poems of this period suggest all my inner turmoil. I had turmoil against Boston and my family. I had turmoil in my head about Catholicism, and I had turmoil about the War, the Second World War. Catholicism had engendered in me a fierce hostility to communism. I was constantly reading *Spiritual Exercises* by Saint Ignatius Loyola and Saint Augustine's *Confessions*."

Cal suddenly changed the subject from Jean Stafford and Catholicism and the War back to poetry.

"I want to tell you something else," he said. "Never be ashamed of being a fanatic; and as you continue writing throughout your life, please don't ever compare yourself to your peers. A poet has to take his or her poem, like a little paper boat, and float it down the stream of every poem that was ever written. Make it float with Rimbaud, or Rilke, or Baudelaire. Make your poem float with great poets, not just ones that are now fashionable. Do you understand?"

"Yes."

I felt as if liquid music had been injected into my veins. I was learning from the master; I was also learning about his life, and it made me understand his religious poetry. I also knew that Catholicism was a way of getting away from Boston-style Calvinism and the Lowells. In Louisiana with Jean, Cal was creating a new life where he was high with religious ecstasy. Cal, it seemed, needed to give himself always to something he was excited about. First it was Catholicism, although his faith had now lapsed. Then it was to be a conscientious objector, in order to protest war. And now? It was love. For both of us, being in love was a form of religion. We called it, "finding our new lives." We were both obsessed with the miracle of finding each other.

8

Apartment

One morning, Cal said "I have a present for you."

He now looked as if he were a little boy. Cal loved surprises and so did I. He was always bringing me small presents, either jewelry or books or bouquets. I wondered what the present was going to be today.

"It's a book. I want to share my love of painting with you. You know I lived in Italy, and I think it was in Florence that my awareness of how magnificent the Italian Renaissance was really began."

Cal handed me a present wrapped in red shiny wrapping paper. I opened it. It was a magnificent, huge art book of his called *The Golden Age of the Renaissance: Italy 1460–1500*. I almost wept. When I read the dedication on the front page, it said "To my great love and favorite poet." He smiled to see how delighted I was with this gift. We opened the book, and he fell into his charming professional mode. We sat on the couch and opened the big beautiful book.

Cal was always studying. He taught himself most of the things he knew about theater, art, dance, opera, and music by studying books. And now he was passing all this learning and excitement about great art on to me.

"The history of the Renaissance has been a kind of parade ground for great theories. There are monographs, formalist points of view, and so many essays in sociological synthesis that the whole idea of the Renaissance has lost its freshness, buried under the stories of artists, the materials they worked in, and the genres they practiced. Let's just forget all that and look at the beautiful pictures. I hope they will inspire you."

I was so enchanted by my art lesson. In the beginning of the book there was a beautiful reproduction of a ship by Carpaccio.

"He was a visionary," Cal said simply. We turned to the jubilation of da Vinci. "I have a book on his life I want to give you," Cal said. "What was so wonderful during the Renaissance was that symbolical thinking was allowed as a great intensity of vision."

After looking at the book of art, we began holding each other and making love.

Afterwards, Cal said, "Sexuality is the life force. It's what makes me a poet, and it's what makes all great poets. You look like a Botticelli, Butterball," Cal said with tenderness. "I have another surprise, darling," he said, smiling his wry smile. "Tonight I'm putting on my good blue suit, a shirt, a silk tie, and my best shoes."

"Not the moccasins?" I asked. He ignored this.

"And you're going home to your father's apartment to change into an evening gown. I'll pick you up in a limousine at seven. I am going to take you back in time to the thirties, when I was young. We are going to dine and dance at the Rainbow Room. I am going to be holding you on the sixty-fifth floor. It's the most romantic and beautiful room in New York City."

I was thrilled at this idea. I had heard of the Rainbow Room; it was built in the thirties and had an art-deco feeling. It was the famous room that rich people, celebrities, and show people went to to dance. It was on top of Rockefeller Center, and you could walk out to a bar and go on a terrace and see all the lights of the city bursting like electrified lily pads in a Monet painting. I was no longer a beatnik; Cal was turning me into a full-fledged lady, a romantic instead of an angry revolutionary poet.

At seven o'clock I was wearing high heels and a simple white evening gown made out of a silk material. Aunt Jewel sprayed me with her Chanel No. 5 perfume. I had gone to the hairdresser, and my blond-brownish hair was long and shining. I stepped into the limousine. I felt this was the happiest night of my life. Good-bye to all of the misery with Ivry. Cal was now the man I would love forever. When we got to the Rainbow Room, Cal had made a reservation.

"Good evening, Mr. Lowell," the maître d' said.

We walked to our candlelit table. A band was playing foxtrot music.

"May I?" Cal asked with a smile.

He held out his arm. We went to the dance floor. We did a slow foxtrot. Cal held me so close I could hardly breathe.

"This will be the closest I will ever come to heaven," I told him.

"Me too," he said sweetly.

We danced in each other's arms. It was a night of bliss. I wished all the people in my life could see me now. Suddenly my mind flashed back to Cherry Lawn School. I remembered the chemistry teacher who threw chalk in my face. I remembered the Irish chef who tried to rape me. I remembered all the sadistic housemothers. As I danced at the Rainbow Room with Cal, I tried to suppress all my past misery. Why were my boarding school memories like smoke fogging my joy?

Soon we were home at East End Avenue. An inner monologue took place in my head: he never saw my rib cage. I would
be next to him breathing, and my ribs would hardly be visible
but they would be there, shiny under the moon, the polished
bones, and I would watch them go up and down but he would
not see them. He was off somewhere else dreaming of what
would be, dreaming of alarms or the slow waking of the next
day. I don't know what he was dreaming, but blatant as horns
in the dream were my questions. I was sleeping next to Cal.
Fluids of my body were endless as ferns. I contained the ocean
and the river bed.

I slept without waking. And when I woke, I heard the snow
outside the window. What were we doing? We were sleeping.
Our legs touched. But he never looked at my arms. He never
saw my arms. I had hidden them skillfully under a long robe
during the daytime, and I had used them to carry baskets and
books and flowers in great brick pots. I had been housekeeping
and then, before sleep, I rubbed the petals on my palms. And
watched the endless snow fall down. Crystals in the dark and I
wanted to give him the gift of my very cold arms.

9

929 Park Avenue

It was twelve o'clock on a spring night when I came back to my father's apartment at 929 Park Avenue to change my clothes before going back to sleep with Cal on East End Avenue. After I entered the apartment, assuming he was sleeping, I was astounded to see my father in his white bathrobe, proudly stolen from the Carlton in Cannes, waiting up for me. My father had a gun in his hand.

"Daddy, what are you doing?!"

He pointed it toward his head.

"What does it look like I'm doing? I'm going to shoot myself."

"Put the gun down!" I screamed.

Then he started to laugh. It was only a toy gun he had bought as a joke to frighten me, but at first I didn't know he was kidding. That was so typical of my father, show and tell all the time.

"Only joking," he said with a big smile.

Why did I have to have such an overly dramatic, nearly-deranged father? Why hadn't he gone into the Yiddish theater instead of the brick and hotel business? No wonder my mother had left him and married a reasonable, assimilated lawyer who was not a crazy person and hysteric. The Hochman sense of humor came from the Lower East Side. Humor had been the secret of Sidney's salesmanship. The brick business was almost totally Irish. Mr. Kelly, Grace Kelly's father, had been one of my father's Irish buddies. Like Bloom, in James Joyce's *Ulysses,* Sidney was always amusing his Irish customers with Jewish jokes.

"Stop that, Sidney," I said. "Stop playing a combination of Falstaff and King Lear."

"Who's that?" he demanded.

Since my father never made it past third grade, it was impossible to use literary allusions. He had no reference to Shakespeare and had no idea what I meant. Aunt Jewel was sleeping. I knew she had told him of my visit to the Barnetts. Obviously he had heard about me and Robert Lowell. I was sure he felt slighted because I had introduced Cal to my mother before I introduced Cal to him. I took the toy gun and laid it down on the French Provincial dining room table Aunt Jewel had recently bought a month ago at Altman's, in her desperation to create an upper-class environment in New York City and cover up my father's terrible Lower East Side tastes.

"I did everything for you!" my father screamed at me. "I was denied custody by that bitch, your mother. That's right, your mother. I suffered all alone without the daughter I loved more than anything in the world. You grew up without even knowing anything about your father. I sacrificed. I saved. I paid all your bills. Singing lessons, do re mi fa so la ti do. Dough? All the dough I spent on your piano lessons? Your riding lessons? Your speech lessons? Your school psychologist? Your summers in Europe?

Not to mention Bennington College. With the money I spent on all the little extras in your life I could have bought the Waldorf Astoria Hotel. And what did you do to me? At nineteen, you play some prostitute in a stupid play in the Village? Is that what I sent you to Bennington College for? I had to tell all my friends you were the ingenue lead. I was so embarrassed. And then? When the play is finished and I say 'thank God, now she can go to law school,' you run off to Greece without a phone number and then to Israel also with no phone number and get married, without me being at the wedding, to a violinist without two cents to his name rumored to be a con man and a fairy."

"Daddy, Ivry isn't a fairy. He's a distinguished concert violinist."

My father continued his soliloquy on the horrors of being a parental relative of mine.

"I'm old. I need you. Finally you've come home. And what happens? You take up with some married poet who's not even Jewish. I've never had the pleasure of meeting this character, by the way; and then to add insult to injury, you take him to your mother's house in Scarsdale where she's leading her *Leave it to Beaver* life before you even show the respect to introduce him to me. You never show me any respect. Who do I have in the world but you? No one. Only you. My own flesh and blood and no appreciation. You show me no love. No gratitude. No appreciation for all my sacrifices."

I was silent for a moment. Then I threw my arms around him.

"I love you, Daddy," I said.

I sighed. There was always such drama with my father. No wonder I was such a basket case. He continued ranting and raving while sitting down on his new $3,000 green velveteen couch he was so proud of.

By the way, I have to admit that there were a lot of classy people in the building business, but my daddy wasn't one of them. Howie Kinney, one of my father's customers, was an impeccably tailored, upper-class Irishman, who often took my father to the New York Athletic Club for lunch, where Jews were not allowed as members. Daddy always had to tell his crude jokes at Howie's insistence whenever he dragged him to the penthouse for a drink.

"Tell me one more time the insurance joke," Howie Kinney begged.

You could always smell Mr. Kinney a mile away, he smelled of expensive men's cologne and bourbon.

"All right, all right," Sidney obliged.

Sidney was one of the great stand-up comedians who had to be urged to go on stage, but once he was on, he knocked 'em dead. He was a great mimic and a great recorder of accents. He had an ear for every kind of accent, and, like a brilliant standup comedian, his comic timing was perfect. Who knew that America's greatest humorist, America's greatest Jewish storyteller, was Sidney P. Hochman, my own darling daddy?

"The insurance joke," Howie Kinney begged.

Sidney never drank liquor, nor did Aunt Jewel, except on special occasions, as when a top building-materials customer like Mr. Kinney visited the house, which Sidney soon turned from a Park Avenue living room into a vaudeville stage.

"The insurance joke," Aunt Jewel echoed excitedly from her front-row seat.

Aunt Jewel loved "borscht belt boom-boom room" humor, and any joke told by Sidney she appreciated, although she had heard him do the insurance joke dozens of times for Howie Kinney, his biggest fan.

"There was this big church meeting down South, and the pastor said 'My brothers and sisters, tonight we have on the stage three of our blessed brothers from the congregation to sell you insurance. They will each have a short time to tell you why you should choose their insurance product. Our first brother

84

is blessed Rufus Brown. Mr. Brown?' Mr. Brown got up and addressed the congregation. 'Blessed brothers and sisters, if you choose my insurance you will be covered by us from the basket to the casket.' Everyone applauded. He sat down. A lot of the good ladies in their big colorful hats murmured, 'Very good. From the basket to the casket.' The next brother peddling his insurance got up and said in a loud voice, holding out his hands, 'From the basket to the casket? Our company will cover you from the womb to the tomb.' He sat down to great applause and a murmur of 'Womb to the tomb,' and he seemed, by far, the better bet. The third salesman stood up and raised his hand: 'Ladies and gentlemen of this blessed congregation. If you choose me, your money will be better invested, I can assure you. Our company will cover you all from the erection to the resurrection.'"

Sidney had only just finished the joke when Mr. Kinney jumped up from the couch and slapped my daddy on the back, saying, "Sidney, you belong in a nightclub. You're the world's best stand-up comedian."

I remember all those joke fests where Sidney wooed his Irish customers. But now he was not very funny about my not getting serious with Robert Lowell. He continued talking to me in the voice of a dying man. He intended to provoke Jewish guilt in my soul.

"I don't have long to live. You know what a sick man I am. I have heart problems. I'm almost blind. I have asthma and arthritis. I'm not going to live very long. Isn't there any *knockus* I can ever have from my only beautiful daughter? Now you tell me you're thinking of marrying this, whatever his name is, poet."

"Robert Lowell, but how do you know all this?" I asked.

"Don't think I don't have a detective following you," he said dramatically.

"Bullshit, Daddy. You're too cheap to spend money on a detective. You squeezed this information out of poor Aunt Jewel. All right, the fact is I've fallen in love with an older, dignified, and brilliant poet. He's written several books and he's dying to meet you."

"Books? It's bad enough *you* want to write books. You think I want a son-in-law who's a book writer? What kind of happiness am I going to have? I was hoping you'd take over Ace Builders Supply. You're smart. All the salesmen would love you, a pretty, overly-educated girl like you selling bricks. It would be a novelty. It wouldn't take me more than a week to teach you everything you have to know. You're as smart as a whip. You get your brains from my side of the family, thank God. And the Dryden Hotel? It's yours. You could spruce that place up. Get rid of Dorothy Draper's *schmutz* and make it into a little jewel. You could throw out all the tenants who are drunks, like that disgusting old man, that James T. Farrell who you spent time with against my orders. Never mind. I already evicted him. He and his wife moved last month to Broadway, thank God. His rich wife, Dorothy, came back to him, and she has money so now he doesn't have to die in the gutter. Never mind him. You could turn that hotel into a famous place. Wouldn't you like to start a nightclub in the basement?"

"But you've rented the basement to Stella Adler and her acting school," I said. "Remember?"

"Yeah. That was another mistake. All those actors with beards and leather jackets walking through my lobby like mobsters. Her favorite student, that Marlon Brando guy, gives me a pain in the ass. I never saw so much five o'clock shadow. And Stella? She's a real *meshugana* if you ask me. She must have had fifty face-lifts. Who does she think she is? Shirley Temple? She wears little leather white gloves all the time to cover the brown liver spots all over her hands, but she can't fool me. I know an old broad when I see one. The hotel is yours if you want it. If you don't want to take over the hotel, which I can understand because frankly it's a lot of trouble every day with tenants always complaining about something. The boiler breaks, the towels have holes, the ceiling leaks, it's always something. But you, my darling Einstein, with your brains I could get you into Harvard Law School. How? Through Julie Wickler, who made a million-dollar donation last year, and you could zip right through law school and then? My God. The career you could have. I know every judge in this city. You could be a litigator. That's how you make a lot of money. Litigate. You have the knack for public speaking."

My father was sweating now. The toy gun was forgotten. He went from his opera of self-sacrifice to the plans he had for my future. Poor man. He had never known a day of happiness after my mother left him. He wanted, more than anything in the world, for me to divorce Gutless and stay in New York City, living with him and Aunt Jewel in his new ritzy apartment.

"Daddy, calm down," I said quietly. "I am going to graduate school already. I'm studying comparative literature with some of the most brilliant English professors in New York City, like Lionel Trilling. I'm happy I'm there."

"Literature? Trilling? More with the literature? All my friends have children who have turned out to be solid citizens. My best friend Julie Wickler's children are well behaved and sensible. His son, Joe, will one day be a rich lawyer. His daughter, Anne, is going to be married to a doctor. A doctor! Can't you be normal like those wonderful Wickler children?"

"I haven't had a normal life, Daddy," I said softly.

I didn't want to rub it in that I had seen a psychologist at sixteen, who told me I'd had the worst childhood he'd ever heard of, and that same psychologist had told me I would have been better off if my parents had died rather than divorced and given me so many double messages which could make any child schizophrenic. And when I asked the doctor, "What is a double message?", he explained to me: "I love you but I have no room for you in the house," or "I'm coming to see you Sunday" and never arriving, or "just sit here like a good girl and I'll be back after work in six hours" and then forgetting to return and leaving me, a nine-year-old child, waiting in a hotel room for her father to return, a full two days alone. "Those are double messages," he said. "Your parents damaged you by being constantly passive-aggressive." And when I understood that I would always be a damaged person, I thanked the psychologist for tipping me off to the bullshit of my childhood. I was listening to my beloved daddy ranting about how ungrateful I was for a childhood in hell.

It ran through my mind how my group of ten-year-old girls in the Stein House, at Cherry Lawn Boarding School for the demented and unwanted, used to sneak out of the Stein House into the woods, smoke cigarettes, and sing our theme song, which I provided the lyrics for using the German tune called "Tannenbaum."

For you we live!
For you we die!
Cherry Lawn Embalming School.
We do our best to satisfy
Cherry Lawn Embalming School.
Hack hack hack the corpse
For we must find a reason.
God how the body stinks
It must be out of season.

Yes, those were tunes and lyrics of my childhood. Not to mention the fanfare and colorful flourishes of running away from boarding school, being found by the police, getting threats of being expelled. Or my secret experiences of hanging out with a group of rich girls in the Stein House, at the age of eleven, who had managed to steal a stack of forbidden pornographic blue books from the chefs who had a bungalow on campus. Later those books educated our group, called by us "the gang of six," all about sexual positions, and we had to hide the books under our pillows when Miss Elliot, our housemother, came to the outdoor porch where we slept, freezing in our parkas and long underwear, using her flashlight to search the porch like a Nazi for forbidden sexual literature.

All these scenes ran through my mind as I listened to my poor darling Sidney demanding to meet the man, he learned from Aunt Jewel, I now wanted to eventually marry.

"I want to meet him," my father said, now a little calmer than he had been when I entered and found him with a phony child's gun in his hand. And now he delivered another typical double message, which I had gotten used to by now, saying, "I'm sure I'll love him. If you love him, I love him."

And with that parting attempt at unconditional love, he turned around and went back into his bedroom. That night I went to sleep with my usual anxiety about everything in my life. I had the nightmare of being back in boarding school. I stopped being a basket case as I crept quietly to the telephone in the living room. I heard my father snoring in his bedroom, and I knew the coast was clear. I dialed Cal's new phone number.

"Hi," I said.

"Hi," he answered.

"I love you."

"I love you, too."

I hung up the phone and went to my desk. I turned on the lamp. It was now one o'clock in the morning. I had been making notes for poems. I wrote brickyard poems about my father. I spent about three hours revising, as Cal was teaching me how to restructure poems after they were written. I settled finally on the title "Clay and Water." I couldn't wait to show it to Cal the next day. We had both decided we would give each other a poem as a wedding present. This was the one I thought Cal would like:

CLAY AND WATER

In my father's brickyard
I saw walls of brick around me. Bricks

Bricks, so bright they were,
One piled upon the other
Like small red suitcases left in the Gare St. Lazare.

I stood in my father's brickyard
And I wondered where I came from, or if
There was something I could ask him,
Something that we would not stumble on.
—Climbed to my father's office.
Covered with white dust, there were files,
And a desk—and there! My father, curious
As I to know why I had come.
Then I asked him, "Tell me about bricks,"
Thinking that he certainly
Had something about bricks to tell me.
"What is there to tell?"—"About bricks,"
I insisted, "about their names."
He looked through
Papers on his desk, all disarranged,
And asked Mr. Bard, his partner, who
Didn't know; and finding nothing to tell,
He said, "Bricks come from clay and water.
They come from water and clay."

Later, when I walked into the yard,
I looked up and saw my father waving at me.
Standing like an old man
Cemented in the strong window of life.

Cal had taught me, through *Life Studies,* how to make use
of my family as material. For Cal, everything was material.
Everything was grist for the mill, including the mill itself.

10

Pillow Talk

O ne night, after I cooked one of Cal's favorite dinners of poached salmon, we were sitting on his bed listening to classical music. We both loved listening to opera records that transported us into a magical soundscape.

I told Cal, "Since you love opera so much, I feel that in the future, you should be writing not only plays, but also try your hand at opera librettos."

He agreed that he would try very soon to investigate the possibility of getting a commission to do that. Since Cal was a literary celebrity, considered by many to be the most important American post-war poet, after T. S. Eliot, it wasn't hard for him to get commissions or grants for any creative work he wanted to do. One of his qualities I loved was that Cal was extremely generous. He was trying to convince the Guggenheim Foundation to give a grant to Elizabeth Bishop, who was living in Brazil and always seemed to be short on money. Cal received countless requests from various students and old friends for help in getting grants from foundations, and he was extremely thoughtful and put himself out to help everyone, for whom he could write recommendations, to secure extra money. He was aware that being a Lowell and receiving money from a family trust fund gave him a financial privilege that few other poets had.

One night I said, "I still don't understand why your friends at St. Marks School called you Caligula. Why did you admire the Roman tyrant Caligula so much?"

"I had a collection of toy soldiers, and I always took an interest in tyrants. Caligula was a mean son of a bitch and so was I. I was often belligerent, and you know I was very big and strong and a lot of boys were afraid of me."

"Afraid of you?" I said, surprised. "That's hard to imagine, when you are always so gentle."

Cal replied, "Not always. I have my really dark moments when I go into the labyrinth of the dark night of the soul. I get really angry at everything and everyone without knowing why. It's almost as if I become another person."

"A dysfunctional childhood may be behind that. A spiritual flu," I said with compassion. "A childhood lacking love and understanding never goes away. Your parents made you powerless against their wishes. After all, they held the purse strings. When your parents, descendants of the Puritans, did not approve of your choices of women or of your career, they wanted to shape you into their own mold. Perhaps, like me, you did not want to follow in the footsteps of your parents and you wanted another life for yourself. Our parents are supposed to be role models. God knows I wanted to be a poet, not a bourgeoise. I didn't want to be like my mother, married and living in the suburbs with kids. I was a rebel, not a middle-class lady filled with dreams of worldly possessions. I had read all the plays that my English teacher Mr. Burwell gave me to study, and I think I wanted to be like George Bernard Shaw's Joan of Arc, or better, like Shaw himself.

"At boarding school, I was angry. I was frustrated that I was a girl living in a man's world. All the books, all the art, all the music back then were male creations. What chance did I have to be a famous writer? We never studied women writers, except Emily Dickinson, who was a hermit, or the poetry and sonnets of Edna St. Vincent Millay, who, in my opinion, was a little too sweet. Her love poems suited me when I was twelve, but by the time I was thirteen I had outgrown Edna St. Vincent Millay. Then there was Gertrude Stein. I thought her writing was rather boring and too cute. I never liked her work. I had an eccentric, bald, very old man as a friend in Paris who was always ass-kissing Ivry, Virgil Thomson, who is a composer. He had collaborated with Gertrude Stein on an opera, but I found it boring too. The Brontë sisters seemed pathetic. Virginia Woolf and Pearl Buck were two of the few women writers whose novels were on our library shelves. All the other writers seemed to be men. I knew if I was going to be a writer, especially a poet, I would have to have guts and be very gifted to compete with the literary male world. I was determined to be a writer as good as Virginia Woolf. That's why I never dated, never drank, and never got into drugs at Bennington—because I had a mission, a dream to be a writer. I always knew I had to keep my mind sharp so I could compete as a writer."

Cal nodded.

"So why did you admire Caligula? He was a ruler mostly known for his cruelty, extravagance, and sexual perversity."

Sometimes Cal was silent when I questioned him. As if he had to make up the truth. But not this time.

"I admired power and cruelty. Perhaps I felt that it was only by cruelty I was going to break the mold my parents had

93

imagined would be my life. They had my life all planned out from birth to death, and even my burial was to be with my ancestors in New Hampshire. Everything was planned the day I was born. Harvard University, summers in Nantucket, upper-class girls. I was never allowed to associate with undesirables."

"Were you ever violent?"

"I was, with my father. He was such a weak man, and although he was a naval officer and had the Lowell name—which was so attractive to my mother, who was a Winslow—he was a wimp. In our set you only married into other families like your own, and what they had to have was a pedigree. And what was that? Your pedigree depended on how long your ancestors had been in America, as white people, of course. By the way, the Kennedys were never part of our social set. They were looked down on because they hadn't been in America for more than a generation. The disease of our families was the disease of snobbery. Who came over on the Mayflower? That was the important question. The Cabots, and Wendells and Peabodys and Sedgewicks, and Hutchins and Cushings, that was the in-crowd. To the manor born meant a kind of Calvinist and Puritan reverse grandiosity. One day I had a fight with my father, who was half my size. I wanted so badly to go to Kenyon College in Ohio, which of course was nowhere in his opinion. After one year at Harvard and one summer at a writing conference in the South, I felt I had found the people that really understood me in Allen Tate, John Crowe Ransom, and Randall Jarrell, all Southern writers and soul mates who were all talented and appreciated me and my talent. Randall Jarrell once said to me, 'I always have the excitement before reading one of your poems, Cal, that I am going to be reading a masterpiece.' These poets made me believe in myself for who I was. They approved of me, whereas at Harvard, I was always on the fringes. An oddball who liked Rembrandt. When Professor Ransom got offered a position to teach at Kenyon, I wanted to follow him. My father wrote a letter to me telling me I was not allowed to disgrace the Lowell family by leaving Harvard. My uncle Horace Lowell, a real anti-Semite if there ever was one, was president of Harvard, and I had to stay there. I was also quite angry at my father because he had disapproved of my first girlfriend, Anne Dick. Anne was older than me and quite easy to manipulate, and I was trying to manipulate her mind and get her to study the same books that I was reading with Blair Clark and Robie Macauley and her cousin Frank Parker, who were my three best friends. Frank was the artist who illustrated two of my books of poems. I loved Anne, but my family disapproved of her as they disapproved of every other woman in my life. My father butted into my business and didn't allow Anne to stay very late in my room at Harvard. He dared to write to her parents about what he considered to be her bad behavior."

"So you were angry with your parents?" I asked Cal, looking into his beautiful cat's eyes which had flecks of yellow.

"Yes. Not only angry, but their mediocre minds and their philistine tastes, not to mention their prejudices against Jews and Negroes, made me sick. The day my father forbade me to go to the college of my choice, I knocked him down. And guess what? To my surprise, he then allowed me to go to Kenyon College. It was amazing that he realized I wasn't his personal property and allowed me to do what I wanted, not what he and my mother wanted me to do with my life."

I spoke up. "The difference between you and me, Cal, was that I was very proud of my father. Although he was a diamond that was a little rough around the edges, I knew that my brains came from him and so did my strong sense of self-respect. I was also grateful to my mother because she took me to concerts, opera, and museums. But when I was a little girl, she married a man who didn't want me to live with them. I was hurt and angry. I felt abandoned. But that has passed, all that anger. As you saw in Scarsdale, we are all good friends now. After the

Second World War was over, my father bought a hotel called the Parkside in New York City by Gramercy Park. A few years later he flipped it and bought a larger residential hotel called the Dryden, with his best friend, Julie Wickler. The Hotel Dryden was a very exciting place because many dignitaries from the United Nations stayed there and later Bobby Kennedy had his office there. It was exclusive and old fashioned. The lobby was decorated in old-world society taste by the famous interior decorator Dorothy Draper. The Dryden, like the Tuscany Hotel, which was one block away on 39th Street, was a residential hotel and expensive. My father was still in the brick business, but he enjoyed the prestige of owning the hotel where Nelson Rockefeller came to visit to be advised on business decisions. I have always been very proud of my father, although at times his clownish personality embarrasses me. When my father first bought the Dryden, with Julie Wickler's money, it was understood that Julie would remain in his job of being a first-class New York corporate lawyer and Daddy, with his outgoing personality, his street smarts, and his sense of humor, would run the hotel. When Sidney bought the Dryden, I went with him to the basement, and he went through some old boxes left by departed tenants. You'll never guess what he found."

"What?"

"Believe it or not, dozens of letters that President Abraham Lincoln wrote to one of his generals. There it was, the beautiful handwriting of the greatest American President. And then, believe it or not, Daddy told me, 'I'm going to give those letters as a present to Julie,' as if he had found a box of old biscotti to give away, and I said, 'Daddy, please don't do that. These letters are history. They are priceless. They belong in a museum or the Smithsonian Institute. Don't just give them as a gift. I bet they're worth a fortune.'

"But my father, who knew nothing about American history and even less about the value of Lincoln's letters, insisted on giving them to his best friend as a present. I was so mad at him for not giving them at least to me, if he had to give them to anyone, that I didn't speak to him for two days. But I could never stay mad at my daddy for very long. I loved his jokes and his funny way of looking at the world, and I loved his bizarre and brilliant business genius. You like bears? To me my daddy was like a huggable polar bear.

"When the Dryden was purchased, my father immediately moved into the hotel penthouse. The penthouse was the most enormous apartment I'd ever seen in New York City. It must have been about nine thousand square feet, with a glass roof over the dining room. As we ate dinner, we looked up at the stars. Daddy's penthouse had a huge wrap-around terrace. Before Sidney bought the hotel, the penthouse had been rented to a Hollywood tycoon. There was a large square hole cut in the living-room wall where the movie mogul put the projector when he screened films in his apartment. Daddy furnished the penthouse in the cheapest furniture he could buy second-hand. This was before he met Aunt Jewel. He bought a breakfront for books, but since he never read books there were almost no books in the lovely breakfront. There was just one book that a locked-out tenant had left in the hotel room. Wolfred, the elevator man, had given it to my father. It was a history of Andrew Jackson written by a young Harvard historian, Arthur Schlesinger, Jr., who now advises President and Mrs. Kennedy. That poor book looked so paltry in a bookcase meant for at least a hundred books.

"And in the living room? You wouldn't believe it. A gray industrial carpet that Daddy bought in an outlet store covered the marble floor. There was also a huge, rose-colored, second-hand couch in two parts made of a disgusting shag material. In the enormous living room was another couch shaped like a yellow kidney. You could say my father favored neurotic furniture. And then in front of the first rose couch was

97

a glass kidney-shaped table, a coffee table, with a large green pottery bowl filled with walnuts, and a wooden nutcracker of two women's legs, designed so the legs cracked the nuts. It was disgusting. But my father thought it was funny. On the coffee table was another gimmick: an old-fashioned gun that turned into a cigarette lighter when you pulled the trigger. Can you imagine how I cringed when Lanie Du Pont, a chum at Bennington, came to visit me in New York? She comes from the hoi polloi Delaware Du Ponts, and Sidney at the time was very low polloi. The most bizarre things of all were the paintings. I told you Sidney had no taste whatsoever, and he was thrifty. He still has the first nickel he ever made. When he furnished his magnificent penthouse, he did it on a tiny budget. To cover all the white walls he knew he had to have pictures, so he went to a frame shop that was going out of business, and he bought dozens of gold picture frames, large ones and small ones. The idea was to frame something, but Sidney had nothing to frame. So he kept the pictures already in the frames. And they were all portraits of Negroes, Africans, and interiors of Southern gospel churches. Our entire house, living room, dining room, bedrooms, was covered with portraits, photographs, and etchings of African-Americans. It looked like his apartment might have been the penthouse of Muhammad Ali, or that Daddy worked with the decorator from the NAACP. Some of my friends from college asked me if my father was a Negro. 'I wish he was,' I said. But I loved Sidney because he was a self-made character, a buffoon. He has no talent for anything except making people laugh and making a lot of money. He is a clown, but I love him. What a character, a real original. Outside of you, Cal, my daddy's the love of my life."

Cal mused on what I said. He gently kissed my neck and said, "People in our social set didn't know any Jews or Negroes, they only knew other upper-class, tight-assed Episcopalians. Actually one of my grandparents had married a Jew, but that was rarely talked about. Once, when I was in my only year at Harvard, I invited my Jewish friend from Harvard, the poet Delmore Schwartz, over for dinner. Delmore was the first Jew my parents had ever met socially, and it was comical because they were trying to sound very un-anti-Semitic, but everything came out in malapropisms. Delmore, I believe, never forgave me for that dinner. He was appalled by the servants, maids in white lace aprons with lace caps, and by the food, which was lamb with mint jelly. He felt very unsympathetic to all the right-wing conversation, being a lefty. He was also turned off by the portraits of Puritan and Episcopalian relatives on the wall. Mostly, he felt my parents were snobbish and rude, which under their good Boston Brahmin manner, they were."

Cal and I laughed at all these personal confessions. We couldn't be together very long without making love, and moments later we were doing just that.

Afterwards Cal said, "I have something to tell you that's a secret. Before meeting you, I started to go through a dry period where I couldn't write anything. That's why I wrote *Imitations*. Now that I've met you, I feel like writing again. You've brought something into my life that every poet desires, and that is love, excitement. You're like a beautiful angel bird that flew into my life. Firing up the landscape of my soul as nothing else could. I am so grateful that you have replaced all the sparrows. You are not only a bird, you are my angel of mercy. I need you so I can speak and write in the tongue of angels."

"I need you too," I said.

I lay back in his arms and drank in the perfume of his Bay Rum cologne. Sex was always followed by literary conversation. Outside of J. D. Salinger and Samuel Beckett, writers usually love to talk. I told Cal how much I admired Delmore Schwartz. I loved all his work, and I had once met him. I had visited the home of the novelist Josephine Herbst, and I had told her that Delmore was one of my favorite poets.

"Oh, he's a filthy old man, you wouldn't want to meet him," Josephine Herbst said. But she didn't realize that I did want to meet Delmore Schwartz and I didn't care that he was filthy and old. To me, at seventeen, he was a genius. Later that week I looked him up in the phone book, and found he was listed. I called him up and said "You don't know me, but I'm a poet at Bennington College, and I think your memoir, *In Dreams Begin Responsibilities,* is the best memoir I've ever read. I'd love to meet you."

He was flattered and didn't really care who I was. Delmore was friendly and invited me to come downtown to the Village and meet him at his apartment. I was a little afraid to go there by myself. I thought if he was a drunk, as Josephine Herbst said he was, he could be dangerous. So I asked Aunt Jewel to drive me down and wait for me in front of his house in Daddy's car. I had read all his poetry and his short stories and his account of his parents' disastrous marriage which, of course, form the body of the subject matter for *In Dreams Begin Responsibilities.* That memoir in so many ways reminded me of my own parents' disastrous marriage. I thought Delmore's writing was musical, very much the prose of a poet. And so, to meet him, I climbed four flights of stairs leading up to his morose apartment. I knocked on his door, and he let me in. He was old and dirty and unshaven. But so what? He was a genius. He was a brilliant conversationalist even when he slurred his words. After an hour of talking to me about all the complaints worming into the apple of his soul, he gave me five dollars to run down and buy him a case of beer. Which I did. I knew most of the poems from *Vaudeville for a Princess* by heart and I recited them to him as he drank his cans of beer. He was pleased. But I never saw him again. I sent him a letter from Paris, but it was returned unopened. Wherever I lived with Ivry, no matter at what apartment, I pinned Delmore's poem "Vivaldi" on the curtains, cut from the *New Yorker,* and read it every day to myself. It was my bible lesson for the day to remind me to write poetry and to keep believing in the literary gods that were true saints.

"Shall I recite my poem about Delmore in *Life Studies*?" Cal asked.

"Oh, yes. Yes."

Cal sat up in bed. As usual he was a great orator of his own work.

Even in his striped Brooks Brothers pajamas, reciting poems out loud gave him pleasure, and he wasn't at all bashful about sharing his work out loud.

"Poetry is meant to be spoken," he often told me.

To Delmore Schwartz

We couldn't even keep the furnace lit!
Even when we had disconnected it,
the antiquated
refrigerator gurgled mustard gas
through your mustard-yellow house,
and spoiled our long maneuvered visit
from T. S. Eliot's brother, Henry Ware. . .

Your stuffed duck craned toward Harvard from my trunk:
its bill was a black whistle, and its brow
was high and thinner than a baby's thumb;
its webs were tough as toenails on its bough.
It was your first kill; you had rushed it home,
pickled in a tin wastebasket of rum——
it looked through us, as if it'd died dead drunk.
You must have propped its eyelids with a nail,
and yet it lived with us and met our stare,
Rabelaisian, lubricious, drugged. And there,
perched on my trunk and typing-table,
it cooled our universal
Angst a moment, Delmore. We drank and eyed

The chicken-hearted shadows of the world.
Underseas fellows, nobly mad,
we talked away our friends."Let Joyce and Freud,
the Masters of Joy,
be our guests here,"you said. The room was filled
with cigarette smoke circling the paranoid,
inert gaze of Coleridge, back
from Malta——his eyes lost in flesh, lips baked and black.
Your tiger kitten, Oranges,
cartwheeled for joy in a ball of snarls.
You said:
"We poets in our youth begin in sadness;
thereof in the end come despondency and madness;
Stalin has had two cerebral hemorrhages!"
The Charles
River was turning silver. In the ebb-
tight of morning, we stuck
the duck
-s' web-
foot, like a candle, in a quart of gin we'd killed.

No one ever captured the essence of Delmore the way Cal did in this poem. He knew how brilliant Delmore was, even if no one else did. Cal told me confidentially that he had left his first wife, Jean Stafford, for Delmore's ex-wife, Gertrude Buckman. Cal dropped the relationship because he knew Delmore was still madly in love with her. "I always feel a little guilty about my affair with Gertrude, even though she didn't drop Delmore for me."

Later, when we were smoking cigarettes and Cal was treating himself to a martini, he confessed that Gertrude was bitter and wrote a nasty poem about their affair, which she published in the *Partisan Review*, the magazine she wrote for at the time.

"I met Gertrude Buckman at a party given by Oscar Williams. She was there with her father."

"I've seen pictures. I thought she was really beautiful," I confided.

"What I like about you and find amazing is that you are never jealous."

I looked at him and smiled.

"There's no room for jealousy when you're in love," I said.

Of course I was lying at that moment.

"That's why I feel comfortable with you," Cal said in his wry, boyish way.

To be truthful, at least with my inner self, I was terribly jealous of hearing about Cal's love affair with Gertrude Buckman. I envied her because I thought she was far more attractive than I was with her large breasts, her green eyes, and her quaint peasant-girl-from-Russia look. She wasn't at all my style. I wasn't a country girl. I wasn't tall, aloof, and going to parties hanging out with my father. But I knew that in the dangerous landscape of love, one had to avoid the landmines and tell creative lies. Life wasn't a confessional poem. I wasn't interested in being overly truthful, a bad trait in a woman in love. I wanted a spiritual healing by the *artifice* of truth.

11

Claremont Stables

One sunny day, we were walking down East End Avenue. We loved our new neighborhood. We lived in a red brick nouveau riche building created after the war. But further down East End Avenue were two elegant buildings built before the war, both in 1929, that reflected the elegance of the late twenties. Number 1 East End Avenue had gold sconces, and a stone elegant sculpture of a woman with flying hair over the entrance. It had white-gloved doormen. It was one of New York City's most elegant pre-war buildings.

"This is where we should live after we are married," Cal said. We walked into the entrance of 1 East End Avenue and saw the large picture window in the lobby which looked out on the East River and threw sun into the dark building's lobby.

"I love it," I said as we walked hand in hand back out on the street.

We were filled with dreams of the future.

"I'm so happy," I said, throwing my arms around Cal. "Being with you, Cal, is so different from being with Ivry. It is easy to have an emotional breakdown as a poet. In Paris, in my last year with Ivry, one day I started crying and couldn't stop. I was so frustrated because I was not leading the life I wanted to lead, and Ivry couldn't begin to imagine that I was unhappy with him. No money, and having to pretend to the concert world that we were successful. Keeping up appearances and having to hold in my anger made me crazy. Ivry is always playing around, and I don't mean playing his fiddle," I said with an ironic smile.

"That won't ever happen with me."

I wanted to believe him.

"I believe you're right," Cal said. "We have our whole lifetime to share theater and music and art. I love opera and theater. You can't imagine what my life was like before I met you. I spent a lot of my time with old and aging poets like Delmore Schwartz, who was once so talented and has come to such a terrible end. Failed ambitions had murdered his spirit. And then I met you. Not a line on your face. Not a slash on your soul. When I see you smiling, and looking so fresh and enthusiastic about everything, I want to be with you. Give you everything that I know."

"You've given me so much," I said. "You're my mentor. My lover. My teacher. I love you with all my heart and all my soul."

"Well, I have another surprise for you because I love you so much," Cal said.

Cal was like a child who was generous with his money, his toys, his contacts. His toys were poems, and he loved to play with them—to recreate them, to read them out loud. Sometimes he'd get mad and throw a poem he didn't like on the floor the way a child throws down a doll.

"What's the surprise?"

"I'm taking you right now to a store called Miller's to buy you a riding outfit. I know you've been talking about renting a horse at Claremont Stables and riding in the park. I know you love horseback riding, but you have to look like a professional rider, not a beatnik. I happen to be a good listener," Cal said. "Whenever you talk about Cherry Lawn School you always say that riding horses was the only thing that you were passionate about, other than writing and reading books. It made you forget about your parents fighting over you."

"It's true. I had my own horse. His name was Ho Hum. He loved me. I found in the stable that horses can give you love that human beings are not capable of. I knew I'd love my horse forever. He's dead now."

"Maybe I'm Ho Hum in another reincarnation," Cal said with a smile. Then Cal hailed a taxi. We went down to the lower part of Manhattan to Miller's riding-apparel store. Once there, I was giddy as I tried on jodhpurs, tweed riding jackets, high-collared riding shirts, helmets made of black velvet, and beautiful leather boots.

"I'm buying you the works," he said simply.

"God, Cal, this is so generous of you," I said. "My dad is such a cheapskate; he would never buy me anything as expensive as these riding clothes. They cost a fortune. You really shouldn't buy them for me. Besides, Jews only buy wholesale."

Cal laughed.

"Someday you're going to make a lot of money as a writer," Cal said, as he took a lot of crumpled cash out of his pocket and paid the wildly extravagant bill at the register.

"As a poet?" I laughed.

"You can write anything. Journalism. Plays. Novels. You're the real thing, Butterball. You have a future that is golden."

"Cal, you give me hope. I've been so miserable most of my life. All I want is to be known as a good poet. I had a Dickensian childhood at Cherry Lawn School, where teachers often abused the students. Writing poetry at Bennington gave me a reason to live. I loved Bennington, but then I married Ivry, and he took all my hope from me for any kind of writing future. But you? You've given me the only thing I ever wanted. Hope. Appreciation of my work. How can I thank you?"

"I'll find a way," he said with his sly smile.

At Claremont Stables, Cal sat in the little office with a copy of W. H. Auden's collected poems. He had brought Auden's poetry to read while I went off riding. Before I mounted the horse, I adjusted the stirrups. Then, in my fancy riding clothes, I called out to Cal and asked if he minded waiting an hour.

"I've already plunked down my cash for two hours," he said in his soft voice that I had come to love so much.

"Two hours?" I asked. I was amazed that he was willing to wait for me in a small, smelly room, not minding at all that he was sitting around the stables. Ivry Gitlis, I reminded myself, wouldn't ever wait for me for two minutes. "Are you sure you're okay with this, Cal?" I asked, sitting on the horse, deliriously happy that I could ride off through the park on a two-hour ride.

"Don't worry, I like the smell of the stable," Cal said. He looked at me through his black-framed glasses. "This is the most fun I've had in ages. I like this place even better than a Newport country club."

He was right at home with the stable boys coming in and out of the tack room. He liked chatting with strangers. I mounted the beautiful brown chestnut horse. Nobody had ever seen me dressed so elegantly at the Claremont Stables before. I was usually riding in jeans and old brown loafers. Now I looked like an aristocrat, or at least a true equestrian, with a black velvet helmet and beautiful black leather boots. I rode slowly out of the stable, only trotting when I got to Central Park. Then I cut loose into a gallop. I galloped around the reservoir, past the Tavern on the Green restaurant. As I rode, I thought of nothing, and that was a good feeling. When I got back to the stable, both the horse and I were sweaty. Cal smiled. He had a marvelous afternoon making friends with some of the riding instructors and grooms. He had no desire to actually get on a horse, but he was able to be happy for me.

"This has been the best afternoon of my life," I told him.

He laughed at me.

"Everything for you is always the best. That's what I love about you. Your enthusiasm about everything. I guess that's what it's like to be young," he said with a sigh.

"You're young in spirit," I said. "Do you think you'll ever ride with me?"

"No, thanks. I'll stick to swimming and tennis and writing."

That night, I gave Cal a new poem I wrote about riding in Central Park:

BEFORE YOU GET MARRIED GO RIDING

And you dream of a horse.
Eyes saddle him,
You go carefully next to him
Admiring his muscle formed like your own,
Cup your legs over his body,
Ride him through bed sheets and pillows,
Blankets, walls, and the moon,
Fix toes in his stirrups, legs cupped over his belly,
Your own flesh yoked to his flanks and mind,
Try riding with the ease of loving
As you gallop past deep fields of childhood
Riding past children.

Riding past childhood and death—
Nostrils open and close
As you kick with your baby heels

Over old fields of violence,
Kicking into the sides
Of the horse whose name never matters
As you ride for your life's sake.

I had typed it out for him on the portable Olivetti that was in my office in the living room. He took the poem, didn't add a word, folded it, and carefully put it in a secret place. He wouldn't tell me where.

"I'm keeping it forever," he said before he kissed me.

As we undressed each other slowly and fell upon the starched white Egyptian cotton sheets, I knew I would never forget these blissful moments of our passion. When we made love that night, we both breathed in our true erotic happiness.

12

The Century Club, Dada,
and Memories of Paris

Cal and I often had conversations about what was happening in the world. We both admired President Kennedy, and especially his establishing the Peace Corps in March. Cal was impressed that Kennedy established the Alliance for Progress between the United States and Latin America. One of Cal's closest friends, Elizabeth Bishop, lived in Brazil, and he went to many conferences in Latin America. He thought this was a great step forward in mutual understanding. And yet there was so much happening in the world that was awful, such as the terrible earthquakes in Ethiopia that left thousands dead or homeless. We both were very involved with the war of apartheid taking place in South Africa. And we were both supporters of Mandela, who was in jail. We both contributed money to fight apartheid. Naturally we felt strongly that there should be an integrated South Africa. The papers were filled with the news about the trial of the Nazi Adolf Eichmann; at the same time, the Soviet cosmonaut Yuri Gagarin became the first human in space.

My impending divorce, Gagarin, and the Eichmann trial all merged in my poem "Manhattan Pastures," which Cal helped me revise. Two years later, I was to become the first woman to win the Yale Younger Poets Award with my book of poetry called *Manhattan Pastures*. Cal was now writing poems again, in the tradition of Middle English poetry. He liked to study the metrical ironic lines which he found in T. S. Eliot and Auden, but he also found beauty in the bardic lines of Dylan Thomas and free verse of William Carlos Williams. He told me that he admired "the linguistic flagellation of myself and also of my husband" in "Manhattan Pastures." He saw it as a poem of a young poet observing the modern fallen world. He called "Manhattan Pastures" a political poem, giving way to an illusive, almost haunting irony, which included auto-biographical references mixed with history. I loved that he liked it, and I asked him to read it out loud so I could hear the rhythms. He was a better reader of my poems than I was. His soft, slightly Southern accent was mesmerizing. I often thought that Cal had conscientiously re-invented himself. Instead of being the Boston Brahmin, Robert Spence Trail Lowell, and speaking with a slightly peculiar upper-class accent, he changed his voice from marbles-in-the-mouth high WASP descended from Puritans, to southern. Instead of Robert Lowell, he was "Cal," and, above all, he had turned away from the life of the upper-class privilege he had been born into, to the life of a rather modest man and not a descendant of Puritans. He had several acquaintances who were men of letters such as Louis Auchincloss, a descendant of the Winthrops and Hutchinsons and Puritans, but Cal covered up his background with a sense of humor. Smiling his huge smile, he read out loud:

Manhattan Pastures

On our wedding day we climbed the top
Of Mount Carmel. To keep our promises
We lay down in maize.
Who can tell us how to lead our lives?
Now in Manhattan pastures I hear
Long processions of the compact cars
Nuzzling their gasoline.
The day is springtime. Have I come too late
To hear the Zen Professor speak of peace?——
"One thing is as good as another," he says, and eats
Salad, wheat germ, and all natural foods.

Voices out of records: terrible sounds.
Wagner's music is a tongue.
My radio announces man in space. This
Was once my city. Who will tell us
How to lead our lives?

Eichmann stalls in the judicial stables.
His children saddle him to a black horse.
Motoring through six million beds of grass.
He wears a light-wool suit tailored for summer.
The doctors say that we are doing well. We shall
Be cured of childhood if we keep
Counting our nightmares in the fields of sleep.
I shear black cars and records in my sleep.

Eichmann drops as man is shot in space
Out of a popgun. In our universe
A lonely husband needs a hundred wives. Who
Can tell us how to lead our lives?

Looking back now, I see that whatever ghosts Cal had in his closet, he kept them carefully to himself. Everyone was very secretive about the mental problems Cal had, because Merrill Moore felt it was not helpful for Cal to have rumors of that kind circulating around him. But at the height of our affair, to me, Cal seemed perfectly normal.

Cal behaved like a charming gentleman, and I kept thinking that he was the best poet in America. His anti-Stalinist views, which came out quite often, had a great deal to do with the fact that he and Mary McCarthy and James T. Farrell had attended a conference where they confronted the fact that no one knew that Babel and Pasternak were tortured in the Soviet Union. Cal had questioned the composer Shostakovich on how the criticism of the Soviet government had helped him as an artist. I was one of the few young people that knew from James T. Farrell that Stalin had killed millions of people and destroyed many artists. I also had read *Darkness at Noon,* which was the first book that really gave an insight into the Soviet butchering of millions of people. After reading that book, I agreed with Cal that Stalin was one of the evil people in the world. In a sense, we were compatible politically. We were also horrified by the Bay of Pigs invasion. It was a day that the whole country was nervous that Kennedy was going to get us into another atomic war and possibly blow up the world. Whenever we talked about politics, Cal was always very rational, and he enjoyed the fact that I read all the newspapers, and we could share our ideas. Thank God Kennedy stopped just in time. We went back to loving him.

I was also happy that Cal had started writing poetry again, and he had been steadily at it the past week with his old inspiration and fantastic concentration. He could focus for hours on one line. He was also delighted that he had started teaching at the New School in New York. I went with him to his classes. Cal and I were delirious and happy to always be together, which made each day in New York City a new adventure. Everyone who met us could see we were madly in love. On weekends I would sleep over at his apartment, and we would wake up laughing without any reason other than that we were so happy to be together. Our routine was that we would shower together. I would take a huge yellow sponge and scrub his back and the rest of his body, and he would then wash me down as if we were two bears cleaning each other. This was one of our favorite activities, showering. Cal had an innate shyness that went with growing up on Revere Street in Boston with Episcopalian aristocratic parents who would never dream of walking around naked in their own home, especially when servants could possibly see them, and were, he told me, always uptight about sexuality. So Cal loved the fact than when we were at East End Avenue we rarely wore clothes when we were alone. Our favorite sculptor was Henry Moore. We both agreed that the body was so much more beautiful in its natural form than covered in clothes. I often just stared at Cal's reclining nude, white body with joy and aesthetic appreciation. East End Avenue was our Garden of Eden. A garden that was our own. Cal told me that his late mother, Charlotte, had studied psychology and psychoanalysis and worshipped the psychiatrist and sonneteer Merrill Moore, who for a time was Cal's confessor and psychiatrist, but despite Charlotte Lowell's studies of Freud and Jung, she was very tight-lipped about sexuality. Cal believed Merrill was his mother's secret lover. He told me that when he was a boy, Commander Lowell was afraid of offending him with sex talks, so explanations of sexuality were off limits. Now with me, suddenly Cal felt free. We danced around his apartment often, nude or sometimes wearing huge oversized white Turkish towels wrapped around our waists. One morning during one of my weekend sleepovers, we decided to see an exhibit of the English painter David Hockney, who was painting colorful portraits that were erotic and now showing in a New York City gallery. Homosexuality was taboo in England, but Hockney was defying the censors and bringing his colorful pictures of homosexual men to the world. We both loved Hockney's portraits, and we also admired the brilliant paintings of de Kooning and Jasper Johns and Rauschenberg that were shown at the Castelli Gallery. Johnny Myers, an art dealer, was publishing and promoting poets who he called "The New York Poets," such as Frank O'Hara, Kenneth Koch, John Ashbery, and Barbara Guest. I loved their work because they all seemed to come out of the Dadaist tradition. They were surrealists, but Cal wasn't sure how he felt about their poetry, their calculated zaniness. I loved the paintings of Larry Rivers, who was part of the New York poets' group. Cal asked me to tell him about Dada. I explained that it had originated in Zurich at the height of the First World War, and it had spread to Berlin, Cologne, Paris, and Romania. I told him that Tristan Tzara had become Dada's main promoter and manager, helping the Swiss group establish branches in other European countries besides Switzerland. Influenced by the Dada movement, a number of radically experimental artists went on to change their artistic disciplines. The Dada genre was a genre of absurdity. Artists such as Kandinsky, Paul Klee, Giorgio de Chirico, and Max Ernst became influenced by Dada. Many painters affiliated with the Dada group, in particular the French artists André Breton and Paul Éluard. Duchamp became the Dada king and Dalí soon followed with his own surrealism. In the strict sense of the word, Dada never was a movement but a brotherhood of artists who each had his own understanding of Dada. All of this led to the follow-up movement of Surrealism. I took Cal to the gallery in New York where I often went, run by Johnny Myers. He and I loved modern art.

Writing was always a part of our day. We both had a tremendous and active drive to act and create. We both loved to sit at our typewriters and escape into a world of language games and linguistic puzzles and rediscover ourselves from the craze of the world around us to become focused on our inner selves. Yeats said he wanted to write poems "good enough to live in." The same idea applied to us.

For fun, Cal and I often went to the movies. Cal did not care much for Hollywood movies. He was much more comfortable seeing European films, and he enjoyed movies by his favorite director, Antonioni, usually starring his favorite actress, Monica Vitti. We saw *L'avventura* three times. Cal claimed it was his favorite. Cal and I also enjoyed going to the Metropolitan Opera. We both loved opera. It took us into another world where the real world disappeared and the world of *bel canto* brought us closer to heaven.

One day Cal invited me to meet him for lunch at the Century Club. The Century Club was the New York City bastion of old waspy values, the essence of polite waspdom for men of achievement. It was the anti-Dada club in New York. I made sure to dress conservatively in a little black dress with pearls. I could barely hear the conversations when we entered the dining room. Everyone conversed in low and polite Episcopalian voices. I couldn't help but compare the old-world Century Club to the outrageous Beatnik coffee shop of the West Village where I wanted to take Cal to hear the great Allen Ginsberg read *Howl*. That coffee house was a place where beatniks and hippies, filthy anarchists, bearded poets, commies, and revolutionaries of every stripe screamed at each other, wore desert boots and filthy jeans, and every other expression was "fuck you" or "bullshit." Louis Auchincloss would not have felt at home in the East or West Village. Nobody wore handmade shoes or shirts with gold pins. I had also taken Cal to "happenings," which were artistic Dada performances that were just beginning to take place in New York. "Happenings" were held in lofts. Comparing the "happenings" and the coffee houses to the all-male Century Club of old-world achievement was a lesson in literary contrasts. Rienzi's and other poetry hangouts often smelled of pot, sweat, arguments, vibrant ideas. The Century Club smelled of polite men's cologne and overcooked asparagus. Laminated facial expressions were everywhere. I experienced the Century Club, this all-male bastion of authors, artists, and amateurs of letters and the fine arts, established in 1847, as a place of refinement. Cal's sort of cronies. It was a temple of old artistic New York, a place of men of old-time soft voices and taste. Previous members, Cal told me, included the editor and poet William Cullen Bryant, and the distinguished American painter Winslow Homer. The club, he told me, evolved from an earlier organization, the Sketch Club, founded in 1821. It was not a place for weirdos. I could sense that Cal, despite the fact that he was an American original and, in my eyes, the greatest poet alive, felt much more at home at the Century Club with the cooked food writers than he would at Rienzi's beatnik coffee shop or the Actors Studio where nobody would recognize him or know who he was. He preferred the Century Club. There, Robert Lowell was a celebrity, a Brahmin with other men of manners and accomplishments. Cal led me over to a table where an old man with the most wrinkled face I had ever seen, droopy eyelids, and perfect table manners sat eating with a much younger man. To my amazement, the man was W. H. Auden. The younger man was his lover.

"Wystan, I'd like you to meet a talented young poet, my fiancée Sandra Hochman," Cal said.

"Pleased to meet you, Miss Hochman," Mr. Auden said, getting up from his chair and speaking in upper-class English.

Then Cal introduced me to Chester Caldman, Auden's companion. He was a friendly and good-looking man who smiled at me with tremendous warmth as he shook my hand. Auden looked like a distinguished high Church of England professor, having lunch with a chubby young Jewish man, the token Jew at the club.

I felt blood rush to my head and, for the first time in a long time, I was blushing. Why? Because W. H. Auden, like T. S. Eliot, had been one of my gods at Bennington.

So this is the famous W. H. Auden? I thought to myself as he shook my hand and looked into my eyes.

Suddenly, I realized that I'd had no idea his W. stood for Wystan.

"How do you do, Mr. Auden?" I said with obvious awe.

"Wystan," he corrected me gently.

I had first come upon W. H. Auden's work when my teacher, Mr. Burwell, at Cherry Lawn, had suggested I spend my vacations from my progressive boarding school at the Public Library in New York City. Excitedly, I had sat, as a teenage girl, for hours reading and digesting the absurdist play *The Dog Beneath the Skin,* written by W. H. Auden and his collaborator Christopher Isherwood. Mr. Burwell said the play would be a very good influence on me. The play was absurdist and poetic. I loved it.

After reading *The Dog Beneath the Skin,* I went on to read Auden's poetry. Auden differed from his Modernist predecessors such as Yeats, Eliot, or Pound. Those poets wrote in free-verse style, an extension of the vernacular. All of this Auden rejected. For Auden, who was political, the pastoral past had been ruined by industrial landscapes and, finally, anxiety and war. Just as Robert Lowell was, in some ways, a poet of personal hardships, Auden's poems not only celebrated moments of personal pain and intensity but also borrowed, at times, techniques from the music hall and the café. In his own public statements, Auden, like Cal, had a sense of consciousness that the poet must have, in order to proclaim a hope for universal harmony. Like Robert Lowell, I knew that Auden often revised what he had written at an earlier period. "Auden is the first poet writing in the English language who feels at home in the twentieth century," I remembered Mr. Burwell telling me. "He brings into his poetry all the disordered conditions of our time, all its varieties of language and events." What seemed to be a paradox to me, as a young poet sitting in the huge New York City Public Library, reading Auden's poetry from his various periods, was Auden's revival of the poetic forms and meters that Modernism had pronounced dead. His rhymes and meters, I thought, only made his poems better. I thought Auden was able to make rhymes and old-fashioned forms as effective as they had always been.

Auden's poems often had an English civility as well as a sense of humor, and were, in some way, like Cal's poetry. I had studied W. H. Auden's life and learned that Shakespeare, and later Goethe and Brecht, had influenced his work. Many years later, when I arrived at Bennington, I taught myself rhyme by copying the rhyme scheme of Auden's poem "Law Says the Gardener Is the Sun." In my first real poem called "Bittersweet," which was published in *Silo,* the college literary magazine, I had imitated the rhyme scheme used by Auden. By trying to imitate Auden, I had taught myself poetry.

"It's so nice to see you, Cal," Auden said, laughing and hugging Cal, who was so much taller than he was.

Chester Caldman popped up from his seat and echoed Auden's delight in seeing Cal. It suddenly occurred to me how similar Cal and W. H. Auden actually were in their careers. I thought this idea through as I stood greeting him at the Century Club. Auden, I recalled, had begun his career as an anarchist, writing with communist Bertolt Brecht in a brashly threatening manner that soon flip-flopped public orthodoxy— mainly Christianity. Cal had also been a rebel poet who became a Catholic fanatic and preached Catholicism on soapboxes in Boston, who then turned his talent in another direction and in *Life Studies* became a secular clown. Neither poet was afraid to be religious or vulgar or personal, nor attempted to address serious issues, such as love, as well as public responsibility; and both of them had a wide range of beliefs and forms. Before I had discovered the poetry of Lowell, I had been in love with the poems of W. H. Auden. Both men were brilliant and had contributed so much to the poetry of the English language. Now I was standing between two of the most imposing poets of the twentieth century. I was thrilled to be there. Auden could not have been more gracious, a gentleman, and, despite his British reserve, a down-to-earth and warm man of letters. Since Cal had introduced me as his fiancée, there was now a buzz of scandal, quietly being whisked around the dining room. Cal, who liked to shock people, seemed to enjoy this buzz. He wanted everyone to know that he would soon be married again.

"Miss Hochman, Chester and I would be delighted to have you and Cal over for tea," Wystan said to me gallantly.

"Oh, thank you, Mr. Auden," I said enthusiastically.

When we walked over to our own table to eat lunch, I felt as if a life-changing experience had happened to me. Meeting the great poet W. H. Auden was almost like smelling a gardenia for the first time. It was an unforgettable experience. Now lines by Auden, from his beautiful poem "Musee Des Beaux Arts," were weaving in and out of my brain:

About suffering they were never wrong,
The old masters: how well they understood
Its human position: how it takes place
While someone else is eating or opening a window or just
Walking dully along:

"Will we really go and have tea with Wystan and Chester?" I asked Cal, my eyes opening with excitement.

We sat down at our table.

"Of course," Cal said, ordering a martini.

"Cal, you promised to give up martinis," I said, reminding Cal that drinking wasn't good for him.

"All right," he said, and he smiled. "You're allowed to look after my health since you are going to be my wife."

He ordered a beer instead.

"Where does Wystan live?" I asked.

"Wystan lives in a smelly broken-down apartment stinking of garbage and moldy books on the Lower East Side," Cal said. "It's cluttered with old newspapers and knick-knacks. It's a mess. Too bad Wystan doesn't have someone, a nice girl like you, to clean up after him, Butterball."

"I'd love to be his housekeeper," I said.

"No, you're my housekeeper forever, remember that," Cal said.

He seemed not really to be joking. We went home to our East End Avenue love nest. Cal seemed so happy that afternoon. He was a very social person, and he wanted the word to get around town that he was starting his new life with me. He released my guilt about our affair by assuring me that he was getting along very well with Lizzie. She had now "gotten used" to the idea that they were divorcing. My anxiety was washed away by our love.

"Our love is like some miraculous bleach," I said to Cal. "It takes away all the dark spots of our past life and makes everything in our new life fresh and new as clean laundry."

That night I composed the following poem as my gift to Cal in gratitude for the lovely afternoon at the Century Club where I first met W. H. Auden.

The Gold Fish Wife

It is Monday morning
And the goldfish wife
Comes out with her laundry
To shout her message.

There! Her basket glistens
In the sun and shines—
A wicker O. And see how
The Goldfish wife touches
The clothes, her fingers
Stretching towards starch,
The wind beating her hair
As though all hair
Were laundry. Come,
Dear fishwife, golden
In your gills, come tell
Us of your life and be
Specific. Come into our lives—
Where no sun shines and no
Winds spill
The laundry from the rope—
Come on the broomstick of a
Window-witch, fly
From the empty clotheslines
Of the poor
And teach us how to air
Our lives again.

13

Dreams and Memories

We were two dream pickers trying to fit the jigsaw of our own lives together in a new puzzle. We had thrown out the old puzzle. And that was what we were trying to do, make our lives start over again. I thought of all this as my dearly beloved Cal snored on his freshly ironed, white, starched pillowcase. I loved him, I thought, I loved him so much. And he loved me too. That was the odd thing. I laughed aloud at our mutual admiration as I fell asleep that night. My life was no longer the nightmare of childhood or my marriage to Ivry. It was a beautiful dream.

"Thank you, God, for Cal," I said as I fell asleep next to him.

The next morning, as I looked at Cal, writing at his desk next to his Napoleon statue, I felt that strange feeling of pride that he gave me when he asked me to read from the galleys of *Imitations*. I read poems from *Imitations* out loud to him over and over every day. Although the book had already been published by Farrar & Straus, Cal still kept rewriting, correcting every line. He was a rewrite freak, but I loved rewriting myself: I knew for him every line had to be perfect, and I was learning from a great teacher to humble myself by rewriting.

As I was lost in the process of rewriting that morning, I remembered staying up all night at Bennington, rewriting my poems. I could revise for hours. I even came up with the phrase: "A poet's best friend is the wastebasket." Cal loved that expression. He had a wry, almost English sense of humor and was always making puns. He loved to twist everything into a joke, and so did I. He often quoted his four-year-old daughter Harriet as if she were a little Oscar Wilde who was much wiser than he was. Cal and I shared an odd sense of humor, and we were often laughing together.

At the apartment, I thought that if I stayed with Cal I would fulfill his needs, not just as a lover but as an intellectual companion, and yes, as a housewife. He would fulfill mine. As a younger woman I could nurture him with energy and enthusiasm about new things. I was praying that the Robert Lowell who had once been so angry and so violent that he knocked his father down on the floor when they fought about his going to Kenyon College was now a person of the past. All of the anger that he had written about was not the Robert Lowell that I now was living with part-time. He seemed to me to be naturally balanced, a bit eccentric, but always cheerful. The teddy bear would soon become a grizzly bear, but I did not know that yet.

"Tell me about Anaïs Nin," Cal said, one night, as we lay in his large king-size bed, watching the news on the television. "How did she come to publish your poetry?"

We turned off the news. It was all bad. It was now the end of May. On May 24, the Freedom Riders were arrested in Jackson, Mississippi for disturbing the peace, after disembarking from the bus. The civil rights movement with its mobs, lynchings, and beatings was in full swing. Cal and I were both disgusted and disillusioned with our country.

"Anaïs Nin? Ivry was in Cuba, and I was alone in Paris. I went to a book signing at an English bookstore. I was taken by a poet, Harold Norse. I had never been to a book signing. The liberation of Cuba was the sensation of the world, and I had been dying to go and meet Castro, Che Guevara, and all the heroes of this miraculous new egalitarian regime. Castro was seen in Paris, and indeed the world, as a glamorous hero who had slain Batista and ended the exploitation of the Cuban people. Ivry and I had argued over the fact that he insisted on going to this celebration in Havana without me. He implied that I would interfere with his action, and he wanted to go alone. I felt angry, left out, and hurt, since I had dragged myself into the pit stops of Greece, Portugal, France, Spain, and England and had arranged for many concerts by giving up my own writing time to devote myself to his needs and demands. Now I was to miss a moment of festivity and history because of his egomaniacal desire to be a star and be a bachelor on the loose, forgetting me. I felt cheated. It was at the book signing where I met Anaïs Nin, who knew right away I was a poet. She was thin and elegant, and her face was that of a Buddha.

"'You're a poet, aren't you?'

"'How do you know that' I had asked her.

"'Do you know that I know a poet when I see one? I tell everything from my intuition,' Anaïs Nin had said to me, smiling. And then, as if I were in a dream, she asked, 'Do you have a book of poetry that I could publish?'

"My face became red. Of course I had a book of poetry. A book of poetry that had been written while I was a literature major at Bennington, and I still secretly wrote poems at night when Ivry wasn't looking. After Ivry became my husband, he more or less locked me into the cage of his own needs and demanded I put every moment of my life and energy into devotion to his career. My book was in a closet.

"'I do have a book,' I said shyly. *How does she know all this?* I thought.

"As Anaïs Nin stared at me and allowed me to talk to her, I was mesmerized. She was a human swan. She had black fingernail polish on her long white fingers. She was thin, dressed in a long white gown, with high cheekbones, almond-shaped eyes, and bright lipstick on her full lips. Her teeth were very white. She wore a sweet Jasmine cologne and a chiffon white scarf around her long neck. She smiled at me in a strange, knowing way. I thought, *I can be a poet again*. I knew Ivry would be out of the picture for two weeks. I could now do what I pleased and meet people who were poets, and writers, and artists, and revolutionaries and had nothing to do with the uptight snobby world of the concert circuit."

"Go on," Cal said. He was a great listener.

"'I will send someone to pick up your manuscript tomorrow morning,' Anaïs Nin said with a Mona Lisa smile, knowing she had the connections and money to do whatever she pleased to help a young poet such as myself. And she kept her word. The next day, to my amazement, Jean Fanchette, a handsome young Mauritian man, rang my doorbell. He explained Anaïs had sent him. He was the editor of *Two Cities,* an avant-garde magazine publishing such writers as William Burroughs and Lawrence Durrell. Fanchette stood politely at my door at 33 Rue Montparnasse asking for my book. Two months later, *Two Cities* published a small edition of one hundred copies of my poems in a book that was blue and white. And that's how my first book of poems, *Voyage Home,* was published."

Cal adored the magical story. He had many stories about his own life to tell me. We had many discussions as we stayed, like gossiping homebodies, in the apartment on East End Avenue. I ended the conversation by saying:

"For me, art is only your own truth. It speeds you from darkness to light. The poet breaks through everything, taking reality and re-conforming it. Who's to say what's real and what is a lie? In the ancient days, primitive men believed in myths. Suddenly, thanks to this goddess, the myth of my boarding-school dreams, to publish a book of poems, had come true. She was my Minerva."

I saw Cal look suddenly sad. But then that mood disappeared, and he seemed euphoric.

"Our love is real to me, too," Cal said as he bent down to kiss me. "Are you still writing your poem, 'Ivory and Horn'?" he asked.

"Yes," I said shyly.

I took out my notebook and began reading to him as he listened to me with his entire attention focused on the rhythms of my new poem "Ivory and Horn" still in the process of being written.

4

I saw a kitten with a tiger's head
Chewing up nine lives. Dead
Sperm lice clinging to his catty snout,
He crawled back to the bag that let him out.
"When you find the Tiger, kill him!" they said.
I could not sleep. I walked about
New York and looked for him.
In the daytime on the park's green lip I stood,
Blood in my mouth flowing like a steam of angry water.
Armed, at night, I ferried the East River,
And pounded on his door. The doorman came,
A blue lion tamer shooing off his game.

5

Snow was falling the first day we walked
Along the river's edge. Rocks
Looking toward Welfare Island seemed a gift

Dropped out of a New England sailing ship.
Gulls followed us in the smoke undertow;
And eye for eye and tooth for tooth and eye for eye
My bridegroom slapped against the river's edge. The
Mayors house was made of gingerbread.
I could not find the straight path out.

6

In Harlem
We climbed the movie steps
That led us to a market place of dance.
We watched a dark brown woman shake in two.
"I am well, I move my arms," she said.
"Never-never dreams wake up the dead."
At the Palladium
Dancing was praising.
Olive ladies
Moved their mattress bodies from the bed
And feather-danced their boys.
Over the wooden dance floor fell
A thousand moving pennies. Catch them all!
Swaying up and down,
No bodies touched, but all bobbed up and down
Jib-shaped and out of water.
I heard the prancing paws of the greased tiger.

7

We crossed Brooklyn Bridge.
In Brooklyn Heights
I heard the sacrament: "You said you meant—
You said you meant—"
Scaled the ice mountains. The
Tiger-eye was strange. I heard claws
Beating in the Stock Exchange.

After I read this section of "Ivory and Horn" to Cal, he turned to me with tears in his eyes.

"This is a beautiful poem. I see the bridge in front of me that found its way into this mysterious poem. It seemed that the Brooklyn Bridge was so many years ago when actually it was only a few months ago. You've changed my life and given me the life I want. We have a wonderful future together. I can't think of anyone I would rather be married to than you. Our love is so beautiful, and I feel so stable and content and productive at the same time."

Soon we were making love. We held each other like two parts of a white marble Henry Moore sculpture. It was as if we fit together perfectly like two pieces in a puzzle. It was as if all our lives we had been looking for each other. What made Cal a great poet? Was it genetics? Was it childhood? Or was it God? What makes someone a genius will always be a mystery.

"The greatest mystery of all is sexual attraction," I said. "But it is a mystery that is divine."

As if reading my silent thoughts, Cal said, "We are like two whales that have been swimming through the dark mysterious bottom of the cold, looking for each other all our lives. Now that we have found each other, it is really so beautiful. Please don't ever leave me," he said.

He said it in a way that was so heartbreaking and yet it made me feel that I had found my mate in the deep black ocean of my life.

14

Political Remembrances

One night after dinner, as we sat drinking brandy out of glass snifters I had given as a gift to Cal for his apartment, I told Cal about how I'd met Gregory Corso in Venice, where I had given a poetry reading with him while my husband was concertizing for Castro in Cuba. I had gone to Venice in 1960 to take part in a collective international manifestation called Anti-Process. I had been invited to go by Jean Jacques Lebelle, a surrealist painter and revolutionary who would, many years later, head the student revolution with Danny the Red on the barricades in Paris. The Anti-Process was a demonstration against what many artists considered the rip-off tyranny of the art world, where the painters, in order to survive, had to pay 50 percent commission to the dealers. Jean Jacques had created a barge for painters and poets to float down the canals of Venice holding placards, protesting the greed of art dealers and the art world in general. This was an exciting media event that was covered by all the global newspapers. There were many leading French international painters and poets arriving from Venice and all over the continent, who interrupted the art fair, using this form of guerilla tactics to get the message to the media. It was Gregory Corso who had asked me to read poetry with him at the Anti-Process, which was floating down the canals of Venice. I remember that Corso had a wildman look in his eyes and gave me a little carved wood angel's head, which I still have. He had probably stolen it, as he was proud of the fact that he had been in jail several times. "I love you," he said, and then ran away and disappeared into the Venice night. He put the angel's head in my hands.

"You have to introduce me to Corso's poems," Cal said.

Gregory Corso's book of poems, *The Vestal Lady on Brattle,* was published in 1955 by the assistants of associates at Harvard where, as a homeless poet, he had been attending classes. *Gasoline* was published in 1958 by City Lights Pocket Press. "Bomb" is one of his most famous poems. Now, back in New York, Corso was reading at a coffee shop in the Village. I asked Cal if he wanted to go. For Cal this was an adventure, and he said yes.

Cal and I went into the crowded reading quietly. I introduced Cal to Allen Ginsberg. Corso read his poem "Marriage":

> *But I should get married I should be good*
> *How nice it'd be to come home to her*
> *and sit by the fireplace and she in the kitchen*
> *aproned young and lovely wanting my baby*
> *and so happy about me she burns the roast beef*
> *and comes crying to me and I get up from my big papa chair*
> *saying Christmas teeth! Radiant brains! Apple deaf!*
> *God what a husband I'd make! Yes, I should get married!*
> *So much to do! like sneaking into Mr Jones' house late at night*
> *and cover his golf clubs with 1920 Norwegian books.*

As Cal got up to leave, I followed him. Many of the beatniks, especially Ginsberg and LeRoi Jones, were poets I admired, but I could tell that Cal was out of his element as the whole beatnik movement was too strange for him. He wasn't interested in the beatniks' energy and subject matter. As we were leaving the café, Gregory Corso recognized Cal. He called out: "I'm glad you didn't read any of your poems, you old fart!" Corso screamed at Cal.

I was stunned by his rudeness. But Cal just laughed as we left the reading. My face was red. I didn't know what to say to soothe his feelings, but Cal was very cool and surprisingly unfazed. Corso had been so disgustingly insulting to the man I knew I loved.

"Beat poets are raw food. I prefer cooked food poets," Cal said.

"That's what I like about New York City. Different strokes for different folks," I said, covering up my disappointment that when it came to the new and exciting beats, Cal and I didn't agree. I decided not to push our disagreement and just keep my mouth shut.

When we got back to East End Avenue, Cal and I entered into a whole new conversation about politics. I told Cal that one of the important features of the beatnik movement was that it was political. Many of the poems were criticisms of American society, especially Ginsberg's.

"Pablo Neruda told me in Paris that a poem is nothing if not political," I said.

"My poetry is political also," he said, "just in a different way. In fact, I really want you to know about the time in my life when I was not just writing political poetry but using my own life as an artist to protest war. It seemed to me being a Catholic that if you followed the Ten Commandments you were against killing, and that led to me being a conscientious objector. I still keep in my files the letters that I wrote to President Roosevelt before being arrested and jailed for being a conscientious objector. Would you like to hear them?"

"Yes, of course."

Cal had brought his portable filing cabinet with him to East End Avenue, and he opened the file drawer and pulled out the papers that had led to his being in prison.

"I must admit that I was in tremendous turmoil. I asked myself, *could the good fight ever be fought with bombs?* I wrote a letter to President Roosevelt."

Dear Mr. President:

I very much regret that I must refuse the opportunity you offer me in your communication of August 6, 1943 for service in the Armed Forces. I am enclosing with this letter a copy of the declaration which, in accordance with military regulations, I am presenting on September 7 to the Federal District Attorney in New York. You will understand how painful such a decision is for an American whose family traditions, like your own, have always found their fulfillment in maintaining, through responsible participation in both the civil and military services, our country's freedom and honor.

I have the honor, Sir, to inscribe myself, with the sincerest loyalty and respect, your fellow-citizen,

Robert Trail Spence Lowell, Jr.

"And then you know what I did? I attached to this letter the 'Declaration of Personal Responsibility.'" Cal then read me the letter.

Orders for my induction into the armed forces on September 8th, 1943 had just arrived. Because we glory in the conviction that our wars are won not by irrational valor but through the exercises of moral responsibility, it is fitting for me to make the following declaration which is also a decision.

Like the majority of our people I watched the approach of this war with foreboding. Modern wars had proved subversive to the Democracies and history had shown them to be the iron gates to totalitarian slavery. On the other hand, members of my family had served in all our wars since the Declaration of Independence: I thought—our tradition of service is sensible and noble; if its occasional exploitation by Money, Politics and imperialism is allowed to seriously discredit it, we are doomed.

When Pearl Harbor was attacked, I imagined that my country was in intense peril and come what might, unprecedented sacrifices were necessary for our national survival. In March and August of 1942, I volunteered, first for the Navy and then for the Army. And when I heard reports of what would formerly have been termed atrocities, I was not disturbed: for I judged that savagery was unavoidable in our nation's struggle for its life against diabolic adversaries.

Today these adversaries are being rolled back on all fronts and the crisis of war is past. But there are no indications of peace. In June we heard rumors of the staggering civilian casualties that had resulted from the mining of the Ruhr Dams. Three weeks ago we read of the razing of Hamburg, where 200,000 noncombatants are reported dead, after an almost apocalyptic series of all out air raids.

This, in a world still nominally Christian, is news. And now the Quebec Conference confirms our growing suspicions that the bombings of the Dams and of Hamburg were not mere isolated acts of military expediency, but marked the inauguration of a new long-term strategy, endorsed and coordinated by our Chief Executive.

Our rulers have promised us unlimited bombings of Germany and Japan. Let us be honest: we intend the permanent destruction of Germany and Japan. If this program is to be carried out, it will demonstrate to the world our Machiavellian contempt for the laws of justice and charity between nations, it will destroy any possibility of a European or Asiatic national autonomy; it will leave China and Europe, the two natural power centers of the future, to the mercy of the USSR, a totalitarian tyranny committed to a world revolution and total global domination through propaganda and violence.

With the greatest reluctance, with every wish that I may be proved in error, and after long deliberation on my responsibilities to myself, my country and my ancestors who played responsible parts in its making, I have come to the conclusion that I cannot honorably participate in a war whose prosecution, as far as I can judge, constitutes a betrayal of my country.

When he finished reading his historic letter, I could see he was proud of being a conscientious objector during the war. Although Wallace Stevens, a contemporary of Cal, slightly older, and from the same class at Harvard as T. S. Eliot, remarked "individual poets, whatever their imperfections may be, are driven all their lives by that inner companion of the conscience which is, after all, the genius of poetry in their hearts and minds. I speak of the companion of conscience because to every faithful poet the faithful poem is an act of conscience."

Cal continued talking a mile a minute: "After a month in which I was treated with almost alarming courtesy, no one questioned my sincerity, I was arraigned before the Southern US District Court in New York and sentenced to a year and one day in the federal correction center in Danbury, Connecticut. While waiting to be transferred there, I spent a few days in New York's tough West Street jail. Then after ten days I was driven up to Connecticut, handcuffed to two Puerto Rican draft-dodgers. At first I was viewed with suspicion by the other Danbury inmates as I had been given a comparably light sentence: the usual term was three years. Jim Beck, an objector, jailed at around the same time, tormented me as he felt that the judge had been lenient simply because I was a Lowell. Beck also berated me but soon saw me as a 'shabby man of God' and decided I was not a fraud. I was made to join a pick-and-shovel gang. The gang walked outside the prison gates each morning and worked on building a barn. My wife Jean was able to visit Danbury for an hour each Saturday. She was receiving $100 a month from my trust fund and was having a hard time surviving in New York. Jean felt it was important to be behind me, although I think she was getting more and more alarmed by my Catholic fanaticism, but in 1944 I emerged from the closed order of Danbury to face the more flexible requirements of parole. As I worked cleaning hospitals, Jean looked all over the countryside for lodgings and found some in Blackrock, Connecticut. So you see, that was how I came to write my poem 'Christmas in Blackrock.'"

"I think that's one of your most beautiful poems and has a powerful alchemy," I said.

"My book *Lord Weary's Castle* appeared in 1947, but most of the reviews didn't start coming out until the following spring."

"While I was reading your book I researched the reviews. I remember what Selden Rodman wrote: 'the voice is vibrant enough to be heard, learned enough to speak with authority and savage enough to wake the dead.' And next came all the honors. I know you won a Pulitzer Prize, a Guggenheim Fellowship of $2,500, and $1,000 from the American Academy of Arts and Letters."

"Those were months of triumph. Around that time, I separated from Jean and went on my own to Washington, D.C., where I became the consultant to the Library of Congress."

Those were Cal's favorite days. That was a very good period in Cal's life, and he loved to tell me about it. He tried to tell me about only the happy memories of his past and leave out the things that disturbed him. He loved to tell me anecdotes about Louis "Lepke" Buchalter, the killer from Murder Inc., who he was jailed with after he was arrested for being a conscientious objector and would later end up in a poem.

"'What are you here for?' Lepke asked me. I turned the question around. 'What are you here for?' I asked him. 'I'm here for killing,' he answered me. 'I'm here for not killing,' I said."

Cal loved to laugh at himself. That was his favorite story about those days and being a conscientious objector.

15

Bear Days

"You know, Cal, the memories I love best are your bear memories," I said.

Cal also loved to tell me about his "bear days." Those were the good ole days at Kenyon College, before all the responsibilities of marriage, earning a living, or being ranked in the list of famous poets (Cal was always wildly ambitious) took its toll on his heart and brain. He made up bear names for his friends and created bear plays. He talked to me in his imitation bear voice. He told me his bear name was "Arms of the Law."

"At first I was rooming with my best friend, Randall Jarrell, but that didn't work out because Randall was so neat and I was so messy. I told everyone what to do."

I had to smile. "Arms of the Law" was Cal's bossy voice. I didn't mind being bossed at all and picking up Cal's filthy clothes from a mess of things thrown on the floor, washing and starching his shirts, taking his things to the cleaners, and shining his shoes. I also considered washing dishes and scrubbing pots good therapy, and in that way we never had any argument at the apartment. It was easy to serve a man who was as kind to me as Cal. Things were going very beautifully in our affair, we were reading poems to each other, we were making love, and since Cal's teaching duties were not strenuous in the New School we had plenty of time to go to the theater, opera, and movies. Cal's favorite director was Antonioni who he considered a genius. We talked for hours about Antonioni.

"You're my mommy bear," Cal often said.

Was I a mommy? Or a film critic? Or was I a sex object? Or was I a younger sister? Or for Cal was I a new buddy? A housekeeper? An intellectual? A new best friend? Was I a student? I felt it didn't matter. I had to play all those roles to Cal. I was enchanted, in our forest of East End Avenue, to be all the women he needed. Wasn't that what love was?

"What I like about you, Butterball, is that you like to help the quick, not the sick." Meaning that instead of being a hospital volunteer, as so many of my old friends from Bennington were, I was helping a genius, and I got spiritual points for that. But what really made our relationship work is that we were sexually perfect for each other. Sex was the glue that kept this collage of poets together.

My father used to kid around in one of his club acts at home, saying "a man wants a cook in the kitchen, a lady in the living room, and a whore in the bed." He elaborated on that idea quite often. "But don't be a fool and get them all mixed up. Don't be a whore in the kitchen, a lady in bed, and a cook in the living room. Don't be a ditz."

Cal told me that with his wife Jean and with his wife Elizabeth Hardwick, he had never really enjoyed sex. He often talked about our sexual relationship in holy terms as if there was some ecstasy that floated from our bodies to our minds to his poems.

"All poets like to be in love, and there's a reason for that. Really great sexual communication is like a shock treatment to the body and the soul. There's a reason that the Elizabethans spoke about sex as a little death."

I wondered if, after sex, comes a sense of humor! Even the sense of the absurd. Cal and I were always laughing. He had a dry, English sense of humor. His conversation was witty, and usually I seemed to share his oddball sense of humor. I loved to make people laugh, and I loved to be funny and so did he. Cal was not only a great poet but a great raconteur. He told me about the time that he visited Bennington College with Elizabeth. She called the Bennington girls "plausible" as if she was talking to an insurance agent. We laughed until we had tears coming down our faces because Cal was now in love with one of Elizabeth's "plausibles."

Cal was nostalgic about Kenyon. "The best thing that ever happened at Kenyon was the college allowing me not to live in a dormitory and putting me and my best friends into a small residence house called Douglas House. We were all young men who wanted to be writers. David McDaniel, Peter Taylor, Robie Macauley. We were shunned by the ordinary boys. We were serious intellectuals, and they just thought we were freaks. Everything was great at Kenyon, but now my Bear days are over," he said sadly.

"No. No. They're not over," I said, laughing at how charming he now seemed to be. He was in a nostalgic mood. He broke into his "Bear voice." As Cal told me his Bear dramas, I couldn't help but think how his symbolic Bear stories might very well have covered up his emotional problems. It was easier to tell me about his sadness in life with Bear stories than in flat-out conversation. Just as I suspected, the great poet Wallace Stevens covered up the tragedy in his life of his being dead to his parents because of his marriage to a lower-class woman, and used his poems as symbolism to cover up his private grief. Cal used his Bear humor to cover up the incidents in his life that were too painful for him to talk about. Instead of talking about knocking his father down and practically killing him, he talked about not getting along with Papa Bear. In a sense, he had to invent his own childish Bear world because the rich boy's waspy life of Kenyon College's jockocracy had nothing to offer him. He became "Arms of the Law Bear." Although he drew his myths of New England, especially in his poem "The Protestant Dead in Boston," the world of Boston, a world without humor, had become a world that Cal now despised. Lawyer? Corporate banker? Cal had never had any intention to follow in that direction, despite the hope of his parents. He would not be what the other young men were going to be, who came out of that Boston Brahmin tradition. He let me know that many of his poems were revenge poems meant to crucify the rich and privileged. The Lowells with their prejudices and Philistine tastes and lack of intellectual excellence had become a world that Cal had learned to distance himself from in Catholicism, poetry, marriage, and now with me, his Jewish fiancée. One of the things that touched me the most about Cal was his tremendous capacity for the love of a friend. There was a kind of glory in his friendship for Elizabeth Bishop. He loved the critic R. P. Blackmur. He loved T. S. Eliot, who he always called Tom, but without a doubt his best friends were Randall Jarrell and Stanley Kunitz. These people were his only family.

As if we were riding magical bicycles in heaven, our love affair was speeding ahead quickly without brakes. Every day was another day that we found out new twists in the past roads of each of our lives. I was curious to know how Cal had created *Lord Weary's Castle*. He told me he had first written *Land of Unlikeness*, which was published by the tiny, unpretentious

Cummington Press. He had rewritten the poems of *Land of Unlikeness* hundreds of times until it became *Lord Weary's Castle*. *Land of Unlikeness,* which he gave me as a present, this slim blue book, and signed to me with love, had the germ of *Lord Weary's Castle.* His St. Marks teacher, friend, and poet, Richard Eberhart, had not liked his changes and revisions, but Cal hadn't listened to him.

"It was Robert Giroux who read the manuscript and urged its acceptance and agreed to bring the book out in the fall of 1946."

Cal said that 1946 was the most important year of his life. I knew that was because it was his breakthrough year as a poet that caused literary people to wake up and take notice of the genius of *Lord Weary's Castle.* As difficult as any book by a modern poet, it won the Pulitzer Prize and rave reviews in America and England. He was only thirty years old.

"Then what?" I asked.

"I guess it was then that I began to think of a symbolic 'Monologue by an Insane Woman' which was really my first wife Jean, which later became my next book, *The Mills of the Kavanaughs.* After that book, I began working on the book you love so much, *Life Studies.* Then came *Imitations.* You see, for me writing a book is just the beginning. You don't write, you rewrite."

And that is perhaps the greatest lesson that Cal taught me. People often ask me what it is like to live with a genius. My only answer is that every day and every moment you learn something. I learned from Cal that every book can be improved. He was never finished with any poem.

Cal was a genius on the one hand, but he was also a child on the other. Like my favorite painter Picasso, Cal was not only creative but childish. "But that is a good thing," I said to myself. "To be creative, you have to never lose the child inside you."

"Let's go to Central Park and ride the carousel," Cal said one day with great lightheartedness.

I was happy. I was tired of only doing grown-up things. At the Central Park carousel, to hurdy-gurdy music, like laughing children we each climbed on a painted wooden horse. The tinkling music began. A stranger or an angel, looking down from heaven, could get an aerial view of a handsome older man in his forties holding the carousel pole above a painted wild horse, and in front of him, riding another horse, was a girl in her twenties with her hair flying. We posted up and down as the carousel went around and around.

"Where are we riding to?" Cal asked me, raising his voice as the carousel went round and round with our horses made of painted plywood. The music was repeating and repeating as we went round and round. The park was filled with wild flowers and green grass, and the smell was so lush that it was overwhelming. We were both so happy being children.

"We're riding to divorce land!" Cal yelled back. "I can't wait till we are both divorced and married to each other."

After we got off the carousel, we walked to the boathouse in Central Park. Cal ran into an old friend from St. Marks, a stuffed shirt who asked if he was there with his daughter. "No, with my fiancée," Cal said, and introduced me. The old boy seemed to wither in his suit because of his *faux pas*. "Don't tell anyone," Cal whispered, knowing the next day it would be gossip. At the Boat House we ate hot dogs and decided to row on the pond where people were rowing like they were in an impressionist painting by Renoir. Cal was delighted. We rented our own little rowboat. Now I felt as if I was in "The Drunken Boat" of Arthur Rimbaud's poem. The sun was shining and as Cal paddled the oars, I could see how strong his arms were. He still had the arms of an athlete. He was wearing a light blue polo shirt that I had given him as a present the day before. And to me, he was a beautiful friend and lover and athlete all at the same time. So handsome, and yet casual, as we rowed into the pond, I could tell he was enthusiastic, as I was, to be starting what he called "his new life." We chatted when the boat lay still in the waters, and Cal pulled in the oars. He looked so happy.

"Tell me about the poet Ezra Pound," I said. I was curious about all his relationships.

"I began to visit Ezra Pound quite regularly at St. Elizabeth's Hospital. He was locked up for being crazy and siding with Mussolini during the War." Cal paused. "He wasn't crazy, just misinformed."

Cal was part of a committee to petition President Kennedy to get Pound released.

"His poems are beautiful," I said. I was a Pound fan.

I continued. "His dictum to 'make it new' guided me in all my writing. It helped me discover my own voice."

"I love Pound," was all Cal said.

The water threw sunbeams from its blue ripples.

That day as we were rowing in Central Park, we stopped the little rowboat in the middle of Central Park Lake. We breathed in the fresh air and continued chatting. Married to Ivry, I had been so nervous and depressed. Now I had found the perfect man, and I felt as if my marriage to Ivry were years ago in another place, another world. I didn't miss him at all. I felt married to Cal.

"Why did you leave your husband?" Cal asked, reading my thoughts as he often did. Cal did have a sixth sense of what was on my mind. I preferred to hear about his past rather than my own.

"It's too long a story," I said.

"Well, make it short and tell it to me," said Cal.

Now he was "Arms of the Law," and I had to listen to his command. I wondered if he was jealous. When he wanted to know something, he could be very demanding, but in a harmless way I had grown to love. He never liked me to look at any other man but him, but that didn't bother me. I was in love with him.

"Let's not talk about the past, let's talk about the future," I said.

Cal didn't fancy dropping the subject so quickly.

"Who is better in bed?" he asked. "Your husband or me?"

"You are," I said.

"Good," he said.

At least I was telling the truth this time. I always told Cal what a fabulous and considerate lover he was, and he felt the same way about me.

A week passed. It was a week away from Passover, the Jewish holiday. Cal was deliriously happy that I had agreed to make a Seder for him. He had never been to a Seder. He was anxious to learn more about Judaism. I was hardly the person to teach him. I had a Lutheran background. But it sounded like fun to explore the Seder with him.

"I want to know what Judaism is," Cal said.

"What's to know?" I said in the voice of a female comedian. "One word sums it up. Mitzvah."

"Mitzvah? What's that?"

"It's doing a good deed." And then I added, "Without anyone knowing about it." Then I added, "Nobody but God."

"In that way it's the same as Buddhism where you're supposed to 'make merit'," Cal said. "Make a Mitzvah for me." Mitzvah now became his favorite word. "Make me a Passover. After all, it was the last meal Jesus ever had, I would like to know what it is like. I'm learning so much from you. I'd like to learn more about being Jewish from you."

"I'm the last person to learn from. I'm not at all religious, Cal. But I do have a beautiful book on Jewish spirituality. I can bring it over and we can read it together."

He was happy.

16

Jewish Spirituality

At night, I read to myself from my small holy book of Jewish spirituality which a reform rabbi, Rabbi Gore, had given to me as a gift, and I read it for wisdom. It was my own private *Catcher in the Rye*, Cal's favorite book, as he had told me before.

"Read it out loud to me," Cal said sweetly. "Go on."

He was interested in anything I was reading. I began to read a passage I loved, "Changes."

> *We are not today what we were yesterday; and what we were yesterday, we were not the day before. Physically, our entire organic structure replaces itself every seven years. In life itself we are constantly changing our roles. One day we are children, soon we are adolescents, then spouses, parents, and so on up the ladder of life. If there be any fixed rule about life, it is that change and flux is its chief characteristic.*

We must understand this basic rule of living and accept the changes within us as individuals and within society.

We must learn to taste to the fullest and enjoy to the utmost the present role we are enacting. It is a part assigned to us for a limited number of performances. Let us seize the moment, before change gives us another role in life.

The main business of a rational society is the business of living with change, comprehending it, and if possible, making it subordinate to the human situation.

"You're educating me," Cal said and held me in his arms.

I was learning about Judaism while I was teaching Cal. My parents were not religious, but they were high holiday Jews. So this feast of the Seder was a treat for me also. Cal loved the intellectual idea of Judaic rules for a better life, and he had an aesthetic approach to everything. *Everything* gave him material for his poetry. Not only the Jewish tradition interested him, but also the terminology. He was, like all poets, in love with words. I explained that the nights of the Seder, or *Pesach,* were engaging, enlightening, and entertaining. The Haggadah, which was the holy book of the table, presented a dialogue between parent and child, leader and facilitator. I explained to Cal that the really lively *Pesach* was not a rote reading service to zoom through, but was rather a drama at the table where people played creative roles. The purpose of the Seder was to remember the story of the Exodus. Since I was almost totally ignorant of the holiday (except that I loved all holidays, especially Christmas and Easter), I was going to choose a short Seder of half an hour, focusing on what I remembered from the Seders I went to as a child at my maternal grandparents' house. I also did some research. I explained the overall structure of the Seder to Cal. The Haggadah was built around four cups of wine for four major sections. The first cup, I explained, was called the *Kiddush,* and the evening opens

150

with this first cup and the sanctification of the holiday by initial invocation with appetizers. A prayer is said over the first cup of wine, and that prayer is called the Kiddush. The second cup of wine, called the *Maggid,* involves questions and storytelling and is the longest part of the Seder. The last cups of wine came at the end. Cal listened carefully to everything I was saying. He loved wearing the yarmulke I gave him. What the hell? Cal was now a Puritan, Boston Brahmin, lapsed Catholic, and Jew. In other words, a poet.

"You'll see when we have the Seder how we ask questions. The third cup is the blessing. After telling the story of Exodus and eating the foods that represent the journey from Egypt, people sing songs of liberation from slavery in Egypt under the Pharaoh."

In Cal's small but cheerful kitchen I began cooking and prepping dinner for the holiday. I previously had celebrated the Seder with my father and his friends, but now I would spend the Seder with Cal, who was to be my future husband.

"What are the symbolic foods?" Cal asked me, fascinated by the upcoming holiday.

He loved to watch me creating magical, symbolic food for the holiday. He wanted all the details.

"First, there is matzo on the table, symbolic unleavened bread since the escaping Jews had no time to bake before fleeing to the desert for freedom. The matzo was to last them in their journey in the desert. Then, on a small plate one places parsley that symbolizes spring, salt water that symbolizes tears, horse-radish is the *maror* which symbolizes the bitterness of Exodus, and all these foods are symbolic and put on the table and eaten at different times during the meal. The bitter herbs are to make us remember our slave status and also to make us remember the freedom we achieved on this very night in Egypt. As it says in the Torah, for seven days you eat matzo, which is the bread of poverty and prosecution, to remember that we were slaves in Egypt. The tradition is all who are hungry, all who are in need, share the *Pesach* meal, where the poor and rich are equal. The most important thing is that the Seder follows the Biblical tradition of hospitality. And I remember, most of all, the wonderful thing about the Seder was that as a child I was taught to ask the *Four Questions*. It was just like a Greek play where the leader asked the questions and the chorus recited the answer. The leader asks how this night is different from all other nights. The answer: On all other nights we eat bread or matzo, but on this night we eat only matzo. On all other nights we eat all kinds of vegetables, but on this night we eat only *maror* or bitter vegetables. On all other nights we need not dip our vegetables even once, but on this night we dip twice the vegetables in salt tears. On all other nights we eat either sitting upright or reclining, but on this night we recline. But really, the Seder is a night of storytelling. The food is like the Catholic wafers, where you eat the body of Christ. Here at the table, everyone dines on the food of the Jews' escape from Egypt and their survival. The toast *L'Chaim* means 'to life.'"

"So how do you know how to prepare the food?" Cal asked me lovingly.

He stood close to me in his kitchen, fascinated by my preparations.

"Well, I used to watch my grandmother cooking for days, gefilte fish, brisket, sponge cakes. I lived with my mother's parents, the Schumers, after my parents were divorced. I loved Grandma Schumer more than anyone in the world."

"I loved my Grandmother Winslow more than my parents too. I called her Gaga." I realized we were both only-child children who ran to our grandmas for love. "I wish I was Jewish," Cal said with a sigh. "My grandmother's husband's name was Mordecai. I'm writing about him."

"Funny, you don't look Jewish," I said.

We laughed. There was never a man who looked waspier

than Cal. We laughed and laughed until tears rolled down our cheeks. I set the table with starched white linen and newly polished and shiny sterling silver I "borrowed" from my daddy's house. Then we sat down to our Seder for two. We enjoyed the Seder. Afterwards, Cal read to me one of his translations of Arthur Rimbaud that was about as beautiful as any poetry could be.

"Forgive me," Cal said, "but since you were bought up in a Christian school, I really admire that you found time to examine your own religion."

"At Cherry Lawn we learned about all religions. It was a progressive school that, in its philosophy, opened every door to spirituality."

"Lucky girl," Cal said.

"I'm a Buddhist, a Christian, a Jew, a Sufi, a Christian Scientist, a Yogi, a Sikh, a Catholic," I said. "To me it's all spiritual, that's where I want to live."

17

Our Childhood Remembrances

So many changes. I felt that my life was filled with beautiful music, playing on a radio that had lost its static. We sat
together on a bench by the East River. It was a lovely spring
morning. It was the next day after the Seder, and Cal felt so
proud of himself that he had learned something new. Cal, who
was, at forty-three, truly a literary icon, had been fielding phone
calls all morning from many of his famous literary friends. He
had spoken that morning to T.S. Eliot, Stanley Kunitz, William
Styron, Anne Sexton, Mary McCarthy, and the poet Randall
Jarrell. Everyone was impressed by his greatness and the world
seemed to be calling him to make sure that, although the word
was out that he was now separated from Lizzie, he was still in
good form. This morning he seemed to be in excellent spirits.
I had also been on the phone chatting away with my new best
friend, Allen Ginsberg, who, despite being a beatnik or a raw

food poet, Cal greatly admired. We were both in a good mood. Sitting on the bench, we started talking suddenly about Cal's childhood. He told me that the only happy year he remembered as a boy in school was when he was five years old and he attended Brimmer Kindergarten. After Brimmer he, told me, it was all downhill. Cal went to school briefly in Washington and Philadelphia, and when the Lowells moved back to Boston in 1925, it was time for him to go to St. Marks. Cal told me he didn't want to go there. He argued constantly with his mother, Charlotte Winslow Lowell.

He told me: "My educational destiny had been mapped out for me at birth. When I was born, my mother put my name on the registry of St. Marks, the Massachusetts Episcopalian School for boys in our social set. As time approached for me to go there, I would constantly debate with my mother. She told me that St. Marks was a 'gift' and a 'family tradition.' My father was a former student. I remember telling my mother during one of these insane arguments, 'Do you know what I'd like to do instead of going to school?' 'What?' she asked with anger in her voice. I told her 'I'd like to be a fly-fisherman twelve months a year.' She immediately told her dear friend, the psychologist Merrill Moore, that I was behaving oddly. Merrill Moore had patiently explained to her that in order to deal with me, she had to have a sense of humor. In theory, St. Marks was able to provide Boston with an annual supply of bankers, lawyers, and junior executives. Founded in 1865, the buildings of St. Marks copied the gothic cloisters and quadrangles of Cambridge in England and Harvard. Its aim was to be architecturally and overwhelmingly impressive. My hobby was collecting toy soldiers. My favorite reading was military history or the history of high-ranking brilliance. I was a below-average student. It was only in the last two years of St. Marks that I began to see myself as an intellectual. It was at St. Marks where I made two important friends, Frank Parker and

Blair Clarke, with whom I tried to foster a creative spirit. The three of us boys would stay up all night secretly discussing the meaning of life, immersed in translating Homer. In a way, we formed our own alternative academy to St. Marks."

"I know that both of these men are still your close friends. I'd love to meet them. I've seen the beautiful drawings that Frank Parker made in your book *The Mills of the Kavanaughs*. It seems that anyone that ever knew you wants to still be your friend. I envy that. I think you have a capacity for friendship that very few people have. I noticed that you're always writing letters and keeping up with people on the phone."

"Well, to tell you the truth, Sandra, the main enemy of a poet is isolation. Every writer who writes needs literary friends. I was lucky to have met so many wonderful literary people in my life, especially when I was doing the recordings in the Library of Congress a few years ago. But going back to St. Marks, the person who made the biggest impression on me was a poet, my English teacher Richard Eberhart. My mother didn't like the fact that Mr. Eberhart was encouraging me to be a poet. Like many mediocre people, my mother thought being a poet was crazy. And so under my mother's advice I consulted with her friend, the Boston psychiatrist Merrill Moore. I later suspected him of being my mother's lover. He was to play an important part in my life. Dr. Moore had not only studied medicine and psychiatry, but he was also famous for writing many poems in sonnet form. One of his published books was called *Simply M* because it contained a thousand sonnets. These consultations with Merrill Moore, who my mother consulted herself, were all part of my mother's campaign to 'tidy me up.' She was very uncomfortable about my being a poet. She and my father had decided I should go to Harvard, like everyone else in my family.

"My first year at Harvard," Cal continued, "I took up with a girl named Anne Dick who was a distant cousin of my friend

Frank Parker. I was girl-shy, and Anne Dick appealed to me because she was very pretty and a little older than I was. I visited Anne at her grandparents' house, and I asked her if I could become one of her suitors. I gave Anne my grandfather's gold watch to mark our secret pact. She later gave it back to me, but by the time I was seeing Anne I was in quarrels constantly with my parents about my future. I was deep into Eliot and Pound and William Carlos Williams. I began to grope toward the idea of becoming a modern poet myself. I didn't want to go to Harvard. I decided to go to Kenyon and follow my teacher John Crowe Ransom, who you've heared so much about. I wanted to marry Anne Dick. That's when I got into a fight with my father over switching schools and knocked him to the ground. Luckily, Merrill Moore convinced me to apologize to my father, and I did. All that anger, by the way, became material for many of my poems about my father. It was Merrill Moore's idea that I should be introduced to a real writer who might take me under his wing. Merrill Moore arranged for me to be introduced to the great novelist Ford Madox Ford. Ford surprised me, after we met, telling me I was 'the most intelligent person in Boston,' and that was the beginning of my belief in myself." Cal paused. "But now tell me something about your childhood. Who influenced you?"

"Just the way you were influenced by Richard Eberhart, who encouraged you in writing your poetry at St. Marks, I was influenced by a teacher at Cherry Lawn Boarding School named Mr. Burwell who encouraged me to not only write but to read all the classics." Slowly the words came from the deep places of my memory. "As a child at boarding school, I developed the dream of being a writer and one day publishing my books. I wanted to do something meaningful with my life. I considered the great poets my best friends. I felt in my heart that there was nothing more beautiful than the symbolism of poetry, the secret language of poetry. I began to hope that in my own poems I could take flight from reality. My mother, who had won me in the fierce child custody battle, sent me to Cherry Lawn at the age of eight. My father capitulated, and paid the bill. They had no idea how I missed them and especially missed having a home of my own. I missed having affection and a sense of belonging to a family. Being at Cherry Lawn was like being at a very expensive mental institution. Almost every child from the lower school to the upper school was an oddball or a tormented survivor of a disturbed home life. There were children from abusive homes. There were throwaway kids whose parents didn't want them. There were even rich orphans or smart orphans on scholarship. There were students who were deaf and spoke to each other in sign language but no one else. There were ringers, or paid athletes who were there from poor families with strings attached, which meant they had to beef up the pitiful boys football and basketball teams. There were children of European royalty who were dumped at Cherry Lawn because their parents didn't have time for them. I remember there was a very good-looking boy in the upper school who was the son of the premier of Greece. The rumor was that he had arrived in America on his own private airplane. He blew himself up in the chemistry lab, but everybody knew it was a suicide. Most of us came from rich Jewish families who, for one reason or another, couldn't take care of us. We were all hungry for love and attention and, to be honest, there was a lot of promiscuity and kids fooling around in the woods. The only thing that we looked forward to in the upper school was social hour, when for an hour after dinner we danced in the Manor House to records of popular music. All the boys got very excited dancing so close to the girls, and then you noticed that the couple had left the dance floor and you knew what they were doing in the woods. I was a very good dancer, but the dances that I liked most were the rumba and the samba. I remember winning the samba contest in eighth grade with Ted

Blastberg. Although the school had mostly Jewish kids, it was run on Lutheran principles. There was no talk ever of Judaism. The principal was a brilliant, old, and eccentric Swedish historian, Dr. Christina Stael Van Holstein, who was Lutheran. We called her Dr. Stael. She believed that every girl in the school should celebrate St. Lucia's Day, as that was a Swedish Christmas holiday. I remember walking with other girls on St. Lucia's Day singing the Swedish carol 'Santa Lucia's' with halos made out of wooden crowns and candles on our heads. Dr. Stael also believed that children needed the arts to express themselves, and everyone in the upper and lower school at Cherry Lawn was encouraged to write poetry, to dance, to be in plays, to compose music, and to go on Sundays to hear chamber music at Dr. Stael's large house, which had beautiful gardens and was on the campus. It was a very progressive school without many rules. The 'Boy's House' was very modern, a huge white box of a house on stilts, created by an architect who had studied with Frank Lloyd Wright. At Christmas time, Dr. Stael threw a huge party at her lovely home, with smorgasbord, and all the students, even the children in the third grade, were encouraged to drink vodka or Swedish schnapps. Her idea was that making drinking forbidden only made it more exciting, and perhaps that is one of the reasons why I never became, like many other poets, an alcoholic. Since many of the professors were refugees from Hitler's Germany and had taught at universities in Europe such as the University of Cologne, the standard of education was like that of a very fine European university. I remember my history teacher, Mr. Zuber, was very important to me because he made history come alive. He talked of all the ancient Greek kings and queens as if they were part of his own family. I remember him saying, in the third grade, 'Zenobia? She was beautiful.' As if he had actually known Zenobia personally. Dr. Stael was a Swedish outdoor health freak. Part of the philosophy of our boarding school was that fresh air is good for you. As a child, I slept with twenty other little girls on an outdoor porch in the Stein House. I remember freezing in our parkas. And classes? Even in winter, they were held outdoors. Despite the fact that the school was bizarre in this way, what was good for me was that we were encouraged to use our imagination. I still have some of the early poems that I wrote about Cherry Lawn. I was miserable. I only liked the time I spent at the stables, or reading poetry or sections of the Bible out loud during those morning meetings held every morning, even in snowstorms. I think it was in the third grade that I found out that I could write about my own life in poetry. My poetry was my revenge on my parents, who had no time for me. Being without a home, and not living with either of my parents in a real home, was the reason I felt lost. Mr. Burwell became the good father. My roots were planted in literature, not in suburbia where my mother and my new stepfather lived with their new family that I did not belong to."

"Why not?"

"My stepfather didn't want me living with my mother. My mother said 'Grandpa told me if you lived with us, it would ruin our marriage.' But that was just her excuse. The truth was her husband, Joe, didn't really want me around. Not just because he thought I was a brat, but also because he really was jealous of how much my mother loved me."

"He was jealous of a child?"

"He was unable to have any feeling for me because I was the child of Sidney Hochman. He was in denial that my mother had ever had a life before him. He couldn't stand the fact that my mother had a child with another man. So they hid me away in boarding school. I was the child he didn't acknowledge, but whenever I visited them, I could hear my mother begging, 'Please, Joe, let her live with us.' I could hear him slam the door of their bedroom and scream 'Get her out of the house, Mae.'"

"And then what?"

"My mother would come out of the master bedroom, take me in her arms, and cry. She would beg me to understand that she had no choice."

"Did you understand?"

"No. I wanted to live with my mother, I loved her so much; and if not with my mother, why couldn't I live with my daddy? It was because she had custody. As she later told me, 'Your father is uneducated, he never went past third grade, and he's not *good enough* for you to grow up with.' I grew up with freaks and oddballs and kids from divorced homes like mine. It was a horrible childhood, because a lot of our teachers and house-mothers were sadistic. They often screamed at us, or abused us verbally. One kid became blind in one eye because Mr. Volk, the science teacher, threw a piece of chalk at his eye when he fumbled and didn't have the right answer to a question. My upper-school housemother, Mrs. Londe, was a lesbian who always had a cigarette holder in her hand. She was a very cultured woman, originally from Germany, and after she was a housemother it was rumored that she became a prison warden. I can laugh at all this now, but it was not a normal childhood. I don't blame my mother, because she thought I would get a better education than I would at Scarsdale, where she lived with her family, and I now see she was right."

"So you forgave your mother?"

"Of course. I forgave Joe too, who, as you know, I now love. I forgave my father, even though my mother told me he slapped her in the face several times, which was one of the reasons she divorced him. But on the other hand, I'm sure she provoked him by looking down on his lack of culture and his farcical sense of humor. You know what? Nietzsche said 'What doesn't kill you makes you strong.' I came out of that school determined to be a great something or other, a great poet, or a great dancer. And a great mother because I hadn't had one really. I wanted a great family. I wanted to live in a house with love."

"So that's what made you a poet?"

"Yes. All that pain became the sand in my oyster, and the oyster became my soul. And the poetry became the pearl."

"Do you remember any poems you wrote during that time?"

"Two poems come to mind," I said. "'Boarding School,' and 'Twelve Years Old.'"

"Do you really remember them?" Cal asked as we sat on our bench.

"Of course. You know I've memorized every poem I've ever written."

"So have I," Cal said. "Tell me the poems out loud."

"Okay. They tell the whole story."

I spoke the first poem.

Boarding School
Pee-Wee, Tut-Tut, Jumbo-Jelly——all wild
Boys, blond lion girlfriends
Combing out their hair
Scratching with their hands. Are you afraid
Of that? Of what?

Childhood. Gangs
Turning math shelters
Into caves and Miss Fowles
Breaking through Math
Bushes with her whip
Of bright red pencils. Mad

Pavilions. Tennis
Brawls. Umbrella trees.
The empty tables

Of the dining rooms.
Cloak rooms and
The boys
Silent on the assembly porch.
So silent now. Why don't they
Holler and scratch?

I hid in the English
Shelter to recover and weep.
The books were growing
Sticky at the roots. And I hide from
Them. Pee-wee brats

Who tag me in drams, back and forth, back and forth.

"And the second?" Cal prompted.

Twelve Years Old
Hello.
I was a brat
Walking alone with forbidden cigarettes,
Gathering up soiled linen, basketballs, hockey sticks,
Letter from home, odd shoes and all
Things that were institutional

I walked in a nightmare. Walked always near the woods
Escaping authority. Dreaming of being a great
Tap dancer or female comedian. Puffing and thinking,
"No! Acrobatics are best!" as I rose
In the boarding-school sky
And no one was lonelier there on the swinging Trapeze.
Fat brat!
Escaping all the authorities. But it wasn't a dream,

And that was the
Forbidden wood—
Hallooo. Do you see what I mean?
I ran through the deep woods wondering
If I had invented the school—or had it invented me?

When I was twelve
The trapeze snapped. The school
Began to wake up. Why
Think that destiny's more than is packed into childhood?

Cal had a sad look in his eyes.

"I love the poems. I'll make all this up to you," he said and continued holding my hand.

He sat with salt tears rolling down his newly shaved cheeks. It was then that I knew he loved me.

18

The Epsteins

Cal was very social, and he was proud of me. He wanted all his friends to meet me. And suddenly Cal wanted me to go to dinner with him at his friends' house, the Epsteins. Barbara Epstein had been an excellent editor who had gone to Radcliffe and edited the now-legendary *The Diary of Anne Frank*. Jason, her husband, was now an important editor at Random House. But I hesitated. I knew they were close friends of Lizzie's, and their apartment was next door to Lizzie's new co-op apartment on 67th Street. I had no desire to meet Lizzie's good friends. It was the first time I ever said no to Cal, but he insisted, and I gave in. The following year, Barbara Epstein and Elizabeth Hardwick, partially with Cal's trust-fund money, were to found the literary newspaper *New York Review of Books*. I knew damn well they didn't want to see me, and I thought it was tactless of Cal to even suggest my going to dinner with them. But Cal was being the bossy, strong Commander Lowell his father had never been. Cal was smoking cigarettes and watching me dry the dishes with his large, beautiful cat eyes. I had not known, when I first met him, that he often wore contact lenses and that he always had a hard time putting them on. When one of his contact lenses had come out of his eye and he was in the bathroom fixing it with fluid, he went into another one of his convincings from the bathroom. Now I had convinced him to stick to his thick-black-framed glasses.

"You look so handsome in your glasses."

The painful contact lenses became a thing of the past.

"You know how proud I am of you. I want everyone to know we are going to be married and be together for the rest of our lives. My new life is so beautiful."

But I secretly felt that Cal wanted to shock his old friends by being with me. That was the bad boy in him that loved attention.

"Doesn't it bother you that I don't feel like being a pet monkey on display?" I said.

I didn't mean to be difficult, but seeing as our love affair was new, I really didn't want a scene.

"Why not? I love monkeys," Cal said. "And I love you. I want everyone to know that. I adore you."

Cal wanted to constantly show me off to his old friends. I really didn't see why I had to meet these friends of Cal and his wife's at all. It didn't seem fair that he was pushing me to do something I didn't want to do. But in my desire to please him, I said I would consider going to have dinner at the Epsteins.

One night when I was at home with my father and Aunt Jewel and my father had gone to sleep, I confided to Aunt Jewel about my nervousness about being a guest at the Epsteins, Lizzie's good friends.

"Don't make a drama out of this," Aunt Jewel advised me. "Men don't like dramas. They don't like women to be sick and they don't want women to give them a hard time. Go. Look pretty. Wear perfume. Don't make a big deal out of this."

Aunt Jewel always gave me good advice. She was savvy about relationships.

Aunt Jewel knew how much Cal meant to me. Cal had spoken to Aunt Jewel on the phone and told her how much he loved me, so Aunt Jewel was now less suspicious of Cal's motives in seeing me. She knew so much more about men than I did at twenty-five. I had been so naïve when I married Ivry, and now I was so sure Cal was the perfect man. In my twenty-five-year-old mind, Cal was always the most intellectual, the best-read, the sexiest man I had ever known. He had a brilliant mind. He was a great poet. And he was wildly enthusiastic about starting a new life with me. He told me constantly that I would grow to love his daughter Harriet. He insisted that I see his psychiatrist, Dr. Viola Bernard, so I could understand him better.

At Cal's suggestion, I went one spring afternoon to talk to Dr. Bernard. She was a diminutive, red-haired, older woman who looked like a librarian. She seemed to approve of me. I felt as if I had passed a test when she actually smiled at me and shook my hand. Before I left I saw a gleam of hatred in her eye.

I realized now, by some mixed-up miracle, I was deeply in love with Cal and he was also in love with me. At the Russian Tea Room our moment had come when he suddenly recognized me as a woman, not just a young obligation to a friend. By now he had totally forgotten our first meeting in Cambridge in 1956. Now it was five years later, and he suddenly looked at me not as his student, but as a woman that brought him youth and joy. I thought of how one moment can change a person's life. The moment of recognition or epiphany was our sudden burst of sexual attraction at the Russian Tea Room that had led to our being together. Cal was now divorcing. I would soon be divorcing also. And we were together. The reason I didn't want to go to dinner at the Epsteins was obvious: I was frightened that his good friends were going to look at me as a young Hester Prynne in *The Scarlet Letter,* with a big "A" tattooed on my forehead. A girl that was taking Cal away from Lizzie. An enemy. But Cal was urging me to go. He assured me that he and I had a higher consciousness that was above gossip and that nothing, no dinner, no friend, no phony psychiatrist, could threaten his love for me. He was very convincing. I stopped protesting. If it made him happy, I thought, why not go? Now, in memory, I realize how I was made out of silly putty. Cal could mold me any way he wanted. As a genius, he had me enthralled. There was no saying no to the Epsteins, no saying no to anything that made Cal happy. I realized what unconditional love was. I couldn't say no to Cal, because I loved him so much. I hadn't understood about true love before now. He could manipulate me to do anything because I couldn't say no to a genius.

It was a cool spring night when we took a cab from East End Avenue to the Epsteins' apartment. At that time, they lived on West 67th Street in a brown, brick, prewar apartment building, near Central Park West and about two apartment buildings away from Elizabeth Hardwick. Barbara Epstein opened the door. Instead of hugging me and Cal, she looked at me the way you would look at an unwanted peddler. Barbara led us into the comfortable middle-class apartment. I was introduced to her husband, Jason. He was, I thought, like Cal, in his forties. He seemed, like his wife, extremely fond of Cal, but I had the feeling that the Epsteins were looking me over and would later be giving Lizzie all the dirt. Understandably, I felt nervous and very young amongst these older and successful literary people.

Before dinner, and after the obligatory cocktails, Cal insisted on reading one of my poems to the Epsteins, from

Voyage Home. As I listened to Cal reading the poem, I couldn't stop thinking how he had influenced me in my writing. The poem was written at Bennington when I had just discovered his poetry. Cal read:

Voyage Home
Walking to your home
I sink my snow boots in the winter chaff;
I am too old to know what brings me here
Except for fear. Perhaps except for love.
Shall we stalk the living room and laugh
Or hum a little to the phonograph?
Inside my child home was a polar bear
Embracing me. Within this darkened lair
I dream again and blood had bought me there.
Time for a good-night kiss. Let us kiss twice
Before I sail into this night of ice.

"What do you think?" Cal asked Jason. I sat very still, hoping that they would like my poem. I was not prepared for what Jason said.

"I think this poem is terrible," Jason replied.

As he said these hurtful words, he looked me in the eye, purposely humiliating me.

Cal then looked Jason in the eye. He said, "That's what they said about Snodgrass. But he went on to win the Pulitzer Prize."

I had never met anyone so mean and rude as Cal's good friend, Jason Epstein. Cal grabbed our coats from the Epsteins' coat closet. He led me out the front door without saying good-bye. I had been so insulted. I felt as if Jason had spit in my face. He wanted to be cruel to me. And he was. We went down in the elevator in silence. That was the end of dinner with the Epsteins.

"Don't worry, Butterball," Cal said when we were outdoors. "I love your poetry. You have rhythm and cadences in your verse that I wish I had. Someday in the future, Jason Epstein will be

171

forgotten, but your work will be read by everyone who loves poetry. That poem is immaculate, gorgeous. You're gorgeous," Cal said.

I could tell he was as shocked by Jason Epstein's insult as I was.

"Oh, Cal," I said, "it's so sweet of you to believe in me."

He wiped the tears from my eyes. "That is the last time I'll ever see Jason Epstein," he said.

"Don't be silly. He's your friend. He's just loyal to Elizabeth."

"You call a person who insults *you* loyal? You should never stand for anyone not appreciating your work. Anyone who insults *you* insults *me*. I should have known." Cal was very angry and now ashamed of the fact that he had forced me to come to the Epsteins'. In hindsight, he realized it was a big mistake.

"Do you still love me?" he asked.

"Of course."

19

Catholicism and Bears of the Past

Just as you want to be Jewish, I have to tell you that during my childhood I wanted to be a Catholic. The great love of my life was not my parents or even Grandma Schumer, it was my nurse, Helen Cohen, an Irish Catholic woman who was very religious. I called her Nursie. She took me to St. Patrick's Cathedral. In the glow of the church, when I held her hand, I experienced the sacred world of Catholicism. The cathedral smelled of incense. A thrill went through my young body as I was filled with the fragrance. I loved the beautiful glowing candles, the stained-glass windows, and the magnificent singing of the choir influenced me. 'I want to be Catholic,' I said to my nurse. 'I want to go to church with you every Sunday.' She said, 'Don't tell your parents, or they'll fire me.' And so, all through my childhood, I secretly went to church with my nurse. I was so sad that I couldn't have communion, and wear a little white dress, like the other little girls I knew who were Catholic. Later, when I went to Bennington and studied modern poetry with Francis Golfing, I was immediately attracted to your book *Lord Weary's Castle*. Mr. Golfing smoked a pipe during classes. His class was held in the living room of one of the small houses on campus called Stokes House. About ten female students in jeans and old sweaters or flannel shirts sat on the floor. Mr. Golfing passed out sheets of mimeographed Lowell poems for us to read out loud. He was teaching the post–World War II poets. We also had to read Eberhart, Kunitz, Bishop, Jarrell, Berryman, Roethke, Delmore Schwartz. But now we were to study Robert Lowell. I immediately understood your Catholic passion and conversion. I remembered how I had wanted to be a Catholic as a little girl.

"I had read, in boarding school, the New Testament, and about the suffering of Christ over and over in my spare time. I discovered that the word Christ meant truth, and I had begun reading all the Catholic literature I could find. I later read the French Catholic writers, particularly André Gide and Jacques Maritain, and studied with Professor Wallace Fowlie at Bennington. Professor Fowlie taught a course called Catholic Literature. But it was in Mr. Golfing's class where I discovered your poetry, which inspired my Catholic writing. It was passionate and it rhymed. I loved your rhythms and found *Lord Weary's Castle* electrifying, particularly since it was totally unlike the work of any other well-known poet. I identified with your fantastic search for the divine. Each poem was like a bullet that went into my flesh and ripped open my arteries. I felt that you were looking for a victory over sin and that you were trying to get near to the great heart of Christ. Just as Jesus began to preach and to say 'repent, the kingdom of heaven is at hand,' within your poetry I found your search for the kingdom of heaven in a materialistic world. And that seems to be what made your first book, *Land of Unlikeness,* so strong.

I particularly love the poem the 'Fall of Babylon,' which has such a personal rhythm of your own and is such a Catholic poem. Your Christian symbolism points to the disappearance of the Christian experience for the modern world of matter, not spirituality. *Land of Unlikeness* and *Lord Weary's Castle* show your attempt to discover how material progress masks social and spiritual decay. I remember, Cal, that Allen Tate, the poet and your friend, wrote: 'In a young man like Lowell, whether we like his Catholicism or not, there is at least a memory of the spiritual dignity of man now sacrificed to secularization and a craving for mechanical order.' I agree with Tate. I can still remember reciting, to myself, as I walked from my poetry class to the house where I lived, the poem 'On the Eve of the Feast of the Immaculate Conception.' I memorized every word, believe it or not."

Mother of God, burly love
Turns swords to plowshares, come, improve
 On the big wars
And make this holiday with Mars
Your feast Day, while Bellona's bluff
Courage or call it what you please
 Plays blindman's buff
  Through virtue's knees.

Freedom and Eisenhower have won
Significant laurels where the Hun
 And Roman kneel
To lick the dust from Mars boot heel
Like foppish bloodhounds; yet you sleep
Out our distemper's evil day
 And hear no sheep
  Or hangdog bay!

Bring me tonight no ax to grind
On wheels of the Utopian mind:
    Six thousand years
Cain's blood has drummed into my ears,
Shall I wring plums from Plato's bush
When Burma's and Bizert's dead
    Must puff and push
    Blood and bread?

Oh, if soldiers mind you well
They shall find you are their belle
    And belly too;
Christ's bread and beauty came by you,
Celestial Hoyden, when our Lord
Gave up the weary Ghost and died,
    You shook a sword
    From his torn side.

Over the seas and far away
They feast the fair and bloody day
    When mankind's Mother,
Jesus' Mother, like another
Nimrod danced on Satan's head.
The old snake lopes to his shelled hole;
    Man eats the Dead
    From pole to pole.

"Your poetry actually began to influence the way I wrote."
"In what way?" Cal asked.
"I was influenced by the fact that you were almost an addict of Catholicism. It wasn't just a religion for you, it was an addiction of the soul. The same way it was for Saint Teresa of Avila in the thirteenth century, a Jewess converted to being a nun, who wrote not just from her mind but from the

irrational place that ecstasy comes from. It is almost as if you, like Teresa, were searching for a forgiveness that could become the instrument of destroying the guilt of a soulless society. The poem, for me, became a golden bracelet, handcuffing you to God. And after I read your work, Cal, I, too, allowed myself to climb the ladder of imagination which leads to a poem. Do you want to hear a first draft of 'Addict,' which I have been rewriting for several years?"

"Let me hear," Cal said.

"I'll just tell you the first verse," I said.

Addict

In bed I lie still, sweating my life out.
It is with you, the addicts (the mad ones)
That I am comfortable. You the aristocrats
That I underestimated: I spied on your
Misery until I became one of you.

"So when you were reading *Lord Weary's Castle,* you were spying on my misery?" Cal asked.

"No. I was celebrating the fact that you were so passionately addicted to Christ that you became a great poet, answering God's call."

Cal listened to what I was saying, and I could tell he was flattered to know that I had fallen in love with his work when I was so young.

"What pushed you to Catholicism?" I asked.

"Many things. My friend Allen Tate and his wife Caroline Blackman are Catholic. And Jean, my first wife, was a converted Catholic. I was teaching at the University of Louisiana when I converted. I thought Boston-style Calvinism had become my enemy. I needed order and passion at the same time. I saw in Catholicism rules for a better life. Rules that would engender art, not view it with suspicion like my family did. I began reading

Etienne Gilson's *Spirit of Medieval Philosophical Experience*. From there I moved on to the Catholic philosophies of Newman, and Maritain and E. I. Watkin. I was also reading Hopkins's poetry and the philosophy of Pascal. I formed a friendship with a young Catholic student of philosophy, Patrick Quinn. In Louisiana, French Catholicism was in the air and Patrick was part of all this. In 1941, I asked Patrick Quinn to be a sponsor for my baptism in the Roman Catholic Church. After my conversion, I remarried my wife, Jean Stafford, in a Catholic Church. I went to Mass in the morning, benediction in the evening, and said two rosaries a day. After our marriage, I spent a week with Trappist monks. I was much happier with the Trappist monks than I was trapped in my marriage with Jean. I needed creative silence." He laughed at his own pun, and then continued talking. "After my year at Louisiana State University, Jean and I moved to New York City. I took a job at Sheed and Ward, the Catholic publishers."

"And then what happened?" I asked, fascinated by this period in his life.

"My marriage was going downhill. I stopped sleeping with my wife. Jean was drinking all the time. It bothered me terribly that she lapsed, as I had hoped to share our piety. My work at Sheed and Ward, even though it only involved modest copyediting, provided me with a chance for a new extension of my Catholic beliefs. Jean was working for a newspaper down on Mott Street. After that, in the winter of 1942–1943, I was writing *Land of Unlikeness* in a high fever. I felt driven, almost deranged, by Catholicism, and as I flailed around in a mix of mythological and Catholic symbols and references, I think I wrote my most elegant and best poems."

"Everything you've written I think challenges our daily culture of soullessness. I must say there is a reason why you won the Pulitzer Prize at age thirty for *Lord Weary's Castle*. In my opinion, *Lord Weary's Castle* is the best book of poetry in the twentieth century, outside of *The Waste Land* and *Howl*."

"Don't always exaggerate," Cal said.

I often wondered what it was like to be such a great genius. *Time* magazine called Cal the best American poet of his generation, but to me what was amazing was that Cal, like Picasso, went from one creative period to another. At first he was a religious fanatic, then a storyteller. Then he invented a whole new form of poems that seemed like inner monologues meant to shock us into how spiritually empty our lives are in *Life Studies*.

"What I most admire about you is that you use the fervent beliefs that inspired you and your own life to make it into art. Also your beliefs are admirable, although now that we know about the horrors of Auschwitz and the Holocaust and Eichmann, I'm not sure I agree with your position on not fighting World War II."

"What do you mean?" Cal asked.

"That we had to fight Hitler and the Nazis. Otherwise I might not be here to love you."

"Well, I am glad you're here to love me, because I never loved anyone as much as you. And I never will."

The conversation ended in silence. I put my arms around Cal, and he put his arms around me. When we kissed each other it was almost as if we really knew what love was. I had begun reading *The Complete Works of Thomas Merton,* published in Argentina in 1958. Merton expressed a faith transcending the boundaries of culture. The reality in his life is, as he writes, "the reality of God." To me, Robert Lowell heard those same voices that Merton heard in the silence of his monastery, but Cal turned his own voices not into silence but poetry.

20

Painting

A re you going to teach me to paint watercolors?" Cal asked. He saw that I loved making watercolor portraits of him.

"Yes."

"When?"

"Now," I said spontaneously.

Cal went happily from the professor to being my painting student. He was usually the teacher, but now our roles were reversed. I explained how my mother had taken me to the Museum of Modern Art when I was a child and how I loved painting. I told him that at boarding school I was called the watercolor girl because I was always creating portraits of my friends with watercolors. I bought Cal some children's watercolor sets. Blue dots. Yellow dots. Red dots.

"Watercolors are what God used when he created Nature," I said. "To paint is to live again. Watercolors are a meditation, to paint myself across the paper with a thick brush."

Cal was having a new creative experience with me. I saw that Cal loved dipping his brush in water and making colors happen. I showed Cal my own technique, which was using the subconscious to just let my hand create a sunset, a face. He began dipping the brush in a glass of water and feeling what it was like to have all the colors become a portrait or a landscape so quickly. It was like writing a poem with colors. His first watercolor was of the sun setting.

"Rimbaud wrote that words have colors, but if that's true, colors are words," I said.

Cal painted rainbows. I painted his portrait. I told him how I had received a watercolor from the poet E. E. Cummings, who also loved to paint, and now he had one of my watercolors. I watched as Cal, like a child, took so much delight in creating his first picture. It was a sun over a red world. He put in big letters from his pen the name of the picture, "Sandra's Sunrise of Creation," and signed it Robert Lowell. Watercolor painting became our new game.

I held the brush and dragged it across the paper. I created several portraits of Cal.

"Isn't this better than writing? It's so much more relaxing," I said, half joking.

He washed his brush and luxuriated in the joy of being an amateur.

Cal was so intense about poetry that it was as if I had given him a magical way to unwind and still create something beautiful and sensual.

"I love watercolors," he said.

"I love you," I answered.

"Well, you will always be my watercolor girl, the first real love I've ever known."

I had no idea if this was obsessive, true, but I wanted to believe him and so I did. While Cal painted watercolors, I cleaned the apartment. I thought of the activities of the past week that we had shared together. Activities? Bliss was more like it. We were both behaving like lunatics, but we didn't care. Like revolutionaries, we were defying the marriage bonds we had made to other people. Lizzie who? Ivry who? We had washed and hung our spouses out to dry like laundry on clothespins. We both wanted new lives.

Cal loved to play with color. I loved that we could sit and paint watercolors for hours together.

21

Falling in the Water

Cal loved the water. One day we decided to go rowing, one of my favorite pastimes in Central Park. After eating hot dogs, we set out in our drunken boat with Cal rowing. I admired his strong arms. It was a magnificent day. We let the boat idle in the middle of the water. I looked around at the other Sunday rowers. The colors of the hats on the women were all pastels. The white clouds in the sky were inspiring. I felt serene for the first time in my life. Cal was wearing his usual old moccasins. He also wore old pants and a striped polo shirt I had given him as a present. He was the picture of health and good manners. Soon, like a kid, I wanted to try my hand at rowing. As I got up so we could change places, the rowboat turned over and we were thrown into the water, capsized. For one second I got terribly frightened. *My god, what if America's greatest poet drowned?* We were splashing like ducks. Cal, from the water, was able to turn the rowboat right side up and retrieve the oars. We managed to get back in the boat. We were dripping wet and laughing. We hugged, soaked to the skin and happy to be alive together.

"Thank God this is not the *Titanic*," Cal said.

We sat in the sun, trying to get warm and dry.

"I've written another stanza of 'Ivory and Horn,'" I said. "I can recite it for you."

8

Near the tiger's bed, my eyes could see
Lovers dancing ceremoniously.
Gracefully, along the corridor,
Geese in slippers danced the varnished floor
Lovingly, lovingly.

On the white pallor of varnishing,
Ladybirds and clock-o-clays could sing.
Bees spun music on the chrome
Of a basin's sun waxed honeycomb
And jaguars pranced. A chittering toad
Sang to the blue eyes of a hog.
Lovingly.

Lovers, when at last from sweet content
You are caught in a dreaming argument,
You will drowse in grass
Under the sea where swans are bound at last,
Lovingly, lovingly.

Cal was very moved by this part of "Ivory and Horn." We were two crazy poets reciting poetry in Central Park. Sitting in a rowboat, soaking wet.

"If it is the last thing I do, I will see to it that this sequence is published. There is such music in it that it is almost like an Elizabethan song," he said.

We sat back in the boat, laughing. We thought our love would never end.

22

The Actors Studio

Once a week I went to the Actors Studio to sit in on what
was called then The Playwrights Unit. After I graduated
from Bennington, before marrying Ivry, I had appeared as an
actress in *The Iceman Cometh,* directed by Jose Quintero at the
Circle in the Square Theater on Bleecker Street. I had become
friendly with a director, Frank Corsaro, whose production
of Jack Gelber's *The Connection* was one of the best American
plays I have ever seen. I asked Frank's permission to bring
Robert Lowell with me to the Actor's Studio, and he said yes.

Some of the other playwrights in the unit were Jack Gelber,
Jack Richardson, and Terrence McNally, who was rumored to
be the protégé of Edward Albee. Another was Norman Mailer,
who confessed to me that he had always wanted to be a poet.
He had written a play of his novel *Deer Park,* and he was trying it
out in the Actors Studio. Mailer and I had become good friends

when I gave him a signed copy of my book *Voyage Home*. During a lunch break I introduced him to Cal.

"You're a great poet," Norman said to Cal.

"And so is she," he said, smiling at me.

Norman had read my book *Voyage Home*. That was a fated meeting. (Many years later, Cal and Norman Mailer were to lead a march in Washington against the war in Vietnam, and Norman later wrote a book about it called *Why Are We in Vietnam?*) After we left the Actors Studio workshop, Cal and I went to dinner at a small French bistro.

"You mean so much to me," Cal said seriously. "I want to get back to a translation of Racine's *Phaedra* and make it my own play in English."

"You will. I predict you will be writing many great plays in the future," I said. I raised my glass of wine. "Here's to future plays by Robert Lowell."

I felt useful because I was inspiring a genius to try new things. Cal told me he wanted, one day in the future, to also adapt Aeschylus's *Prometheus Unbound*. I felt that the pathos and fragility that I sometimes felt about Cal had totally disappeared. He told me that I was helping him to have a new life. I only hoped this love affair which was too good to be true would last. He was writing. I had already written to Ivry saying I was coming back to Paris to get a divorce. Ivry called every week to try to get me to change my mind. But I was in love. And Cal kept talking about us getting married.

"You know," Cal said, "going to the Actors Studio Playwrights Unit has been one of the most fascinating moments of being in New York City, and I have you to thank for that, Butterball."

23

Dinner with Nancy and
Dinner with Stanley

One evening Nancy Tish, who I thought was a very good friend of mine, came to have dinner with Cal and me in our home. Nancy Tish was a gossip and pushy, but I gave in to her self-invitation for old time's sake. She told me she was dying to meet Cal, and I couldn't very well keep saying no. It was the first dinner that I was making for company. I was elated that I could please Cal with my cooking skills, and the idea of the evening with two much younger women had made him walk around the apartment in an unusually good mood. All the time I had lived in Paris with Ivry, we were struggling for money so I learned to go shopping on the streets of Paris, buying a loaf of fresh bread in one store, vegetables in another, fresh black olives in another store, and then fish in the market, putting all the food shopping into the traditional French string basket that Paris housewives used. And so with my old string basket from Paris, I went shopping in our East End Avenue neighborhood. Instead of all the little charming stores, I went to the supermarket. I bought salmon, which was easy to poach, small red potatoes, baby carrots, and fruit salad. I also bought champagne.

That evening I poached the salmon, and Cal and I opened the French champagne before Nancy arrived. After the champagne, we were both in a good mood. When Nancy entered the apartment, she looked at me with an ashen face and intensity. I knew immediately that this was not to be the dinner I had hoped for. I smelled trouble. Nancy gave me her coat, which I took to Cal's study, and then she began talking to both of us, talking very quickly.

"My mother was talking about you and Cal to a friend of hers, a psychiatrist who knew Cal's psychiatrist in Boston, Merrill Moore. My mother's friend loves to shock with gossip." There was silence. Cal only smiled as if he didn't know what she was referring to.

"Cal, stop lying to her!" Nancy screamed.

"What are you talking about?" Cal asked casually. He was having a great time drinking champagne. "Merrill Moore is a poet and an old friend of mine."

Nancy looked Cal straight in the eye. "Have you told her yet?"

Cal's face became red. He avoided looking at me, and it was then that my uneasiness grew.

"Told me what?" I asked, trying to keep my voice steady.

"You're bullshitting her. You liar. You haven't told her about your shock treatment, and all the times you've been arrested for episodes of insanity," Nancy said to Cal.

Nancy turned away from Cal with disgust and looked at me. She took an index card out of her purse. She was the kind of girl who was constantly making lists and writing notes to herself. I wasn't sure if it was because she was absent-minded, or she simply enjoyed looking like she researched everything. She took her index cards out of her bag and began looking at them.

"Cal has had several breakdowns. Several lock-ups, several episodes. Many breakdowns," she read from her index card. "He was hospitalized in Mclean's. He drove his wife Jean into a wall and smashed her nose. He was hospitalized in Salzburg while teaching a seminar. In 1947, while he was a consultant at the Library of Congress, he tried to choke a female socialite. When the authorities of the Library of Congress found out, they'd already hired him and simply hushed up the whole incident. In fact, everyone has hushed up the fact that Cal is mentally unstable. Probably because he would never have a job at Harvard if the authorities at Harvard knew about his madness."

I felt as if someone had slapped me, but Cal just smiled. I couldn't figure out exactly what kind of smile it was, but it surprised me. It was almost the shy smile of a young boy.

"This is all exaggerated," he said, in total denial of this laundry list of loony bins. "Those are just rumors," he said emphatically. "None of this is true. Those times in the hospitals were just rest cures when I was exhausted. Every writer gets exhausted and needs to rest. Elizabeth Bishop has rest cures all the time—does that make her a lunatic? Everyone is just jealous of my success. She's just making everything up," he said to me.

Nancy got up from the table. "Why are you lying to her?"

She raised her voice considerably, since her recitation of her notes had not bothered Cal. He seemed even amused at her performance as if *she* were mad, not he. While she accused him of being a lunatic, he had a look of gentle sweetness in his face. He looked like a very sane professor, not a guilty man. This infuriated Nancy more. The more he smiled, the angrier she became. She had come to break us up. But she was failing.

Cal stood up in a dignified way. "I've had a few mental lapses," he said. "They're nothing to be afraid of. A few isolated episodes. If I were crazy, as you claim, would I be allowed to teach?"

"And even if he did have some breakdowns, so what? We're terribly happy," I said with a shaky voice. "Cal is the healthiest man I've ever been with."

"I don't call being in and out of mental wards and hospitals healthy," Nancy said. Suddenly Nancy grabbed her hat and coat and went to the door. "You're an idiot to believe his lies," she said. "Don't say I didn't warn you. This man is a madman." She continued screaming at me from the hallway: "Liar!" She kept screaming until the elevator arrived to spirit her away.

"Speak for yourself," I screamed back down the hallway. "And you're a bitch!"

I had tears in my eyes as I cleared the dishes. Cal followed me lovingly into the kitchen and hugged me tightly.

"Don't believe all that crazy nonsense. If I were a lunatic, would I write better than any poet?" He kissed my neck. "If I were crazy, would I be the poet for the Library of Congress?"

He held me tight. I felt a little better. My anxiety was being calmed just by the fact that Nancy's voice had been replaced with Cal's calm voice. He looked me in the eyes. He was so handsome and so sweet, I could never imagine him being any other way. He was, to me, a normal and healthy and somewhat eccentric but beautiful and virile man.

"Nancy is a crackpot. She's just jealous of our love. I swear to you, I'm healthy and normal and those incidents will never happen again. I've had some episodes. Who hasn't? But I'm fine now."

"But why would she tell me all these things?" I asked, confused by what Nancy had said. I'd had no suspicion that Cal ever had mental problems.

"Because she doesn't understand that all poets get excited when they are creating. When I was doing the translations for

Imitations, I sometimes felt I was Rilke or Pasternak. But I'm not that delusional." He continued assuring me that Nancy was the crazy one. "Sometimes you just have to *channel* poets that you're translating and rewriting."

He looked at me with love. He seemed perfectly sane to me. We had experienced many months of bliss and rapture and lovemaking. He was sane and loving. Had Nancy invented these lies to hurt me?

"Please, let's never talk of this again. Let me read you some of my poetry. Forget Nancy. She's not your friend now; she's your enemy. She wishes she could find great love like ours." We moved slowly into the bedroom and made love. "Remember, Nancy doesn't live with a man; you do."

He was so convincing. I calmed down. He was always a gentleman and a well-behaved man. That night, I stayed over at Cal's apartment. After we made love, we stayed up all night drinking coffee, smoking cigarettes, and telling each other about our lives. We could talk to each other for hours.

"Why did you give your friends in college the names of bears?" I asked. That struck me as being somewhat childish and eccentric. But funny, too. A little crazy, but crazy in a good way.

"I just think bears are funny," he said playfully. "You see, I'm a bear and I have a sense of humor but that doesn't mean I'm crazy. You're my butterball bear."

He had a sense of humor, and I knew that many artists had slight nervous breakdowns and rested in hospitals. The same had happened to me in Paris, although I didn't stay in a hospital because Ivry couldn't afford it. The doctors at the American Hospital had ordered me to take nine weeks rest because of stress. Everything was still perfect in our lives, Cal's and mine. Cal was my Angel of the Meridian. I adored him.

Cal was teaching his poetry class at the New School. All his students loved him. What was interesting about Cal was that he read poems by very young poets that he admired in his classroom. He read poems by Sylvia Plath, Fred Seidel, and W. D. Snodgrass. Fred Seidel had not yet published a book, but Robert Lowell thought he was one of the best poets he knew and compared very well with Anne Sexton, who had already been honored with a Pulitzer Prize. He enjoyed sharing the poetry of young people with his class. He chose some of the students' poetry to read out loud, and it meant so much to the students because everyone knew that Cal was a great teacher and a great American poet whose admiration everyone wanted. Cal was very generous in praising his students. One night he included one of my poems that he had revised in his reading, and I sat at the back of the classroom with tears in my eyes. I felt so honored that he included my work with Sylvia Plath and Anne Sexton.

We soon decided to be more social. The poet Stanley Kunitz and his wife, Elise, lived in a small brown townhouse that they owned in the West Village, and invited us to their home. I had written a paper once in 1955 when I was at Bennington on Stanley's poem "Goose Pond." When Cal brought me to meet them, I was at first quiet and shy. I had read many others of Stanley's poems in my modern poetry class at Bennington and loved them. Stanley Kunitz had a face that was distinctively handsome, gray hair, a moustache, and a great smile. In 1961, the Kunitzes were barely in their fifties. We sat in their warm living room surrounded by books and Elise's paintings. Stanley invited me to go with him into his garden at the back of the sitting room. He always wore a black beret. He was bohemian. I immediately adored him.

"Cal is a man of genius, and he's in love. I think you're good for him," Stanley said when we were alone.

I felt suddenly as if I'd had a shot of helium pumped into my heart. Stanley Kunitz, one of Cal's best friends, liked me. All was well. Everything he said made me deliriously happy. At least *one* of Cal's great friends appreciated me.

"You're beautiful and talented. You're young. You're perfect for Cal," Stanley said warmly to me.

"Thank you. I'm sure his other friends see me as a home-wrecker," I answered with a sad smile. "But honestly, he had decided to leave Lizzie before our love affair took off."

"Cal has left Lizzie so many times before, but this time I think he's found the right person in you."

"You do?" My eyes glistened in disbelief.

I was so grateful for Stanley's approval. I wanted to hug him. I wanted so badly to be accepted into the small, magical circle of people that Cal loved. Stanley, and his wife Elise, were affectionate with Cal. I could see why Cal loved them. They weren't tight-assed like another friend of Cal's, Professor Fred Dupee, who I had already met and who obviously didn't approve of me. Professor Dupee was a patrician, and I could tell he disapproved of our love affair. The Kunitzes were warm and loving. To Cal they were almost like family.

"Cal tells me you're pushing him to write poems," Stanley said. "That's good. And now he's even watercoloring. Bravo."

We were looking at all his flowers and vegetables. We were talking softly so Elise and Cal, who were drinking in the other room, didn't hear us.

"Cal and I are going on a fly-fishing trip," I said.

"That would be good for him," Stanley replied.

Every time Cal taught his once-a-week class at the New School, we went to see the Kunitzes. I didn't feel that the Kunitzes were talking down to me. Cal wasn't drinking as many martinis as usual, and he seemed happier than I had ever seen him. I knew of course that Cal only felt comfortable with people who loved his work, and Stanley, who was a decade older and a great poet, was a big fan. Cal told me he often tried his poems out on Stanley. Cal was in his element with a happily married painter and poet. Elise loved him also. I think the Kunitzes were role models of what he wanted us to be. Cal was not a solitary person. He liked talking, and you could see that with Stanley and Elise he was able to talk about poetry, art, and music, the three subjects that interested him most.

"It's good for him to meet a young woman who adores his work," Stanley said.

"Thank you," I said. "That's good to hear."

Elise then took me upstairs to her painting studio. There were dozens of invitations to art openings and museum exhibitions on her bulletin board. Although she was much older than I was, I could tell she remained childlike as many artists do. Her works, abstract paintings with great slabs of color, were on easels. She talked about art critics like Meyer Schapiro. Like her husband, Stanley, she wasn't just an artist but an intellectual as well. She seemed to always be smiling, as if she was having a good time all the time. She and Stanley, you could tell, adored each other. Elise hugged me. I felt as if I had just won the literary sweepstakes.

"You're so good for Cal," Elise said, and then she surprised me by saying, "You've given him a new life."

Afterward, we went downstairs and Stanley showed us his greenhouse, where he grew orchids. I think he was even more proud of his orchids than his poetry. I felt so good to be with them. At the Kunitzes, I felt that Cal and I were a couple. I felt very accepted and comfortable in Cal's world. Nancy and her lies were now forgotten.

24

Dr. Viola Bernard

Several weeks later, Cal suggested that I visit his psychiatrist again. He was seeing Dr. Bernard quite regularly now. She gave him medicine, but he didn't talk about his medication to me and I never questioned him. Our relationship was pure bliss, and if he thought that talking with his psychiatrist about us and taking some pills was appropriate, why not? We didn't talk too much about Dr. Viola Bernard, but I knew Cal visited a shrink once a week. She had started him on valium, but he was obstinate and threw it out.

"Is anything wrong?" I asked. I was concerned about his asking me to see Dr. Bernard with no explanation as to why.

"I just want her to know you're good for me and that we're going to be married," he said. "I've told Lizzie I want a divorce, and Dr. Bernard is all for it. She thinks you're good for me. I want you two to meet one more time. It will help me convince

Lizzie that the divorce is the best thing for all of us. I know Lizzie loves me and even though she's been through a lot of difficult moments with me, she will always remain my best friend—and one day even yours, I hope." That made me feel good inside. I never wanted Lizzie to be my enemy. "I think the divorce will be good for her, too. She can concentrate on her writing, and I know our daughter makes her very happy."

"I often wondered," I said to Cal. "if Lizzie's Penelope and you're Ulysses and you'll always go back to her."

This came out of my mouth without my really thinking about it. I meant it as a joke. It was as if I'd slapped him.

"How can you be so paranoid?" Cal seemed offended. "She knows that it's over between us and she knew it long before I met you. You're not the first woman I left her for."

I felt a relief. I didn't want to be the homewrecker the Epsteins seemed to think I was. I knew that Cal had left Jean for Gertrude Buckman and that Jean had been quite bitter and demanding in the divorce settlement because of his affair with Buckman. And then Buckman became bitter and wrote and published nasty poems about her affair. Cal didn't seem to care about money in his divorce. He was willing to share his trust fund and everything he had with Lizzie. He made quite a bit of money from his lectures, books, articles, and teaching, or so he told me. He was overly generous with everyone.

"She must miss you," I said, as a question more than anything else.

"Oh, no, I mean too much trouble," Cal laughed.

"What about Gertrude Buckman? She's very pretty. I met her once at a party at Oscar Williams'. She was with her father, a rather charming man. But I think she had a father fixation."

I wondered if all this trouble with all his women was why he went to Dr. Bernard. Lizzie had stopped calling the apartment to scream at him. He'd been visiting with his daughter Harriet quite often and was always returning in a good mood, repeating Harriet's stories to me. He found her to be a brilliant and charming little girl. He felt that a stable home with me would be good for all of us.

"I know she'll eventually love you," he'd say to me, "as much as I do."

I wanted to make Cal my whole life, and I knew that meant I'd have to understand his darker side. This is why I found myself at 75th Street and 5th Avenue, outside Dr. Bernard's office. As I sat in her antiseptic waiting room, I read some of the magazines on her little wooden coffee table. From the magazines, I could tell Dr. Bernard was no intellectual. She had copies of *Newsweek*, *Time*, and *Sports Illustrated*. I wondered if she was capable of understanding Cal's poetry and genius. I imagined her to be a politically conservative woman. I wondered if she really liked Cal, or if he puzzled her with his anti-American stances and his genius. She'd only been Cal's therapist since he'd moved to New York. I wondered if he talked about poetry with Viola as he did with his Boston shrink, Merrill, who was actually a poet. And did they talk of me? Cal had often told me his move to New York was a rejection of his old life, Boston, and Lizzie. I was part of the rebirth. But was I?

"It'll all be wonderful," he'd say of the future.

I knew Dr. Bernard thought Cal had a chemical imbalance. But she was also looking to "existential causes for his behavior," according to Cal.

"Lizzie says she encourages my delusions," Cal once said.

He told me Lizzie disapproved of Dr. Bernard, but that he was very fond of her and found his visits enlightening.

"Is that bad?" I asked naïvely.

"No. But I want you to see her again."

I was nervous about seeing her again. I wondered what she had to say as I sat again in the waiting room. Dr. Bernard came out to greet me. I wondered if she colored her own hair. It seemed redder than last time. I had no idea what she was going to tell me, but I prepared myself for great revelations into Cal's inner being. She told me nothing. All I did was chat with her. She knew Cal loved me. The conversation didn't start or end with any revelations.

After the session, I met Cal for a walk. We walked in the joy of a new day. The air was clear. I was in a good mood. Cal began talking of all he wanted to write. His eagerness to write a play had increased since our visit to the Actors Studio. He was like a mischievous boy with all his future plans floating around the back of his head. They excited him. We were celebrating being together and the fact that Cal had given up his contact lenses. The contact lenses had made his eyes very red. Now that he only wore his thick glasses, I saw how beautiful his eyes were. *Clear eyes*, I thought, *are spiritual. They are there for insight as well as vision.* Cal's eyes were filled with soulfulness.

"I have a wonderful surprise for you," Cal told me. "Tickets to Carnegie Hall to hear Haydn's *The Creation*."

"How fabulous," I said.

Concerts could now be pleasure, not just work, the way they had been when I went to concerts with Ivry, and he used the opportunity to try to meet patrons or conductors who could help his career. That night, as I sat next to Cal, the music lifted us into another dimension. The oratorio seemed to be speaking to us not only about the creation of the world but the creation of our lives.

"What interests me is that Haydn was close to Mozart in time and spirit. Mendelssohn too," Cal said. "But Haydn did his best work at the end of his life, did you know that?"

"No, I didn't know that," I answered. He was always delighted by my knowledge of classical music. "I have a feeling your life will be like that too. There's going to be a sense of awe and vastness in your work as you age."

The reason I loved Cal was that he was truly not just a writer but a renaissance man who believed in me and wanted me to be a renaissance woman. Politics? Music? Art? Nature? Dance? Opera? Drama? The more time I spent with him, the more I realized that his inspiring intelligence could be very overwhelming. Like Shakespeare, he knew about psychology, philosophy, the sea, the universe, almost everything. Cal understood the human condition. And, like Shakespeare, he was a natural storyteller. I told Aunt Jewel that night how much I loved Cal.

"Be careful," Aunt Jewel said with all the wisdom of her years. She brushed my long hair slowly, as she sometimes did before I went to bed, and whispered in my ear, "Don't love too much, you never know what's going to happen." She sensed disaster but didn't say so because she truly wanted all my dreams of a home with someone who loved me to come true. I had been badly injured by my parents dumping me in boarding school, and the wounds of my childhood might never heal.

25

Fire Island

One morning Cal was feeling chipper.

"You know what, Butterball? I want to rent a car and drive to Oyster Bay. You'd love my Oyster Bay friends as you love the Kunitzes," Cal said.

"Great. I'd love to go down to Oyster Bay. We can do it next weekend," I said.

"No . . . now!" Cal insisted.

Sometimes he was like Bully Bear, but I didn't care. I was happy because I had heard only good things about beautiful F. Scott Fitzgerald country. Oyster Bay. I knew that my favorite photographer, Horst, lived there. Although Horst was primarily known for his fashion photographs, he had taken a liking to me and over drinks had told me that during the war, to escape the Nazis, he had to live in the woods. It was while in the woods, eating berries, that he began taking pictures of trees. I was privileged to see how he photographed trees as if they were people, or leaves as if they were clothes. His photographs of trees were so beautiful. He wanted to give me one, but I gently refused; they were much too valuable to give away, and I felt privileged just to look at them.

I'd heard that Oyster Bay was a very beautiful place, but we never did get to Oyster Bay. In our budget rental car, we swerved and swayed on the highway, going in completely the wrong direction. Cal couldn't find the right highway to Oyster Bay. Finally, he gave up trying. Instead of Oyster Bay, we wound up leaving our rental car behind and boarding a ferry to Fire Island. We were laughing. We were lost. So what? Being lost was fun.

"I wanted always to go to Fire Island," I said, pretending it was normal that Cal had no sense of direction and could not find Oyster Bay.

But I sensed there was something wrong with him. Cal was upset. He was Commander Lowell and his ship had just docked at the wrong port. He was petulant as a child.

"I hear it's beautiful," I told him, hoping he'd cheer up. "Fire Island. It's supposed to be beautiful."

"You see, Butterball, how God takes care of us?" he said, turning to me. "We have to park the car and take the ferry."

Before we got on the ferry, Cal had several drinks at a nearby bar. I had one beer with him. It tasted good. I was beginning to feel that I was in some kind of weird dream, having seen how Cal had gotten so lost on a highway. Whenever I suggested we turn around and go home, he'd become annoyed.

"But I want to see Fire Island," he said in an irritated voice I had never heard before.

It was dark when the ferry landed in Salt Air, and we began to look for a hotel. Every hotel was booked, and we couldn't get a room for any price. We tried and tried. No hotel room. It had become a very dark night. Stars were out.

"Where are we going to stay?" I asked.

It was past the time of the last ferry. Cal led us toward the beach, where we could hear the sounds of the ocean. There were all sorts of odd people sitting on blankets and small chairs. Police jeeps were patrolling the beach, and it was very cold. We huddled together for warmth.

"I want to go home, Cal darling," I said, getting up from the sand. "Maybe we can find a boat?"

We walked back to the town to check out hotel vacancies. Again we knocked on the doors of several hotels. There were no rooms available. It was now getting very chilly. I wasn't dressed for this adventure. I was wearing high heels and a nice new light blue linen suit.

"We'll have to sleep on the beach," Cal said cheerfully.

"We're not the Marines landing in Normandy, Cal. And I'm not a sleep-on-the-beach person," I protested.

Sleeping on sand was not going to be fun for me. I realized now that my new outfit was appropriate for Oyster Bay but not Fire Island.

"It's a great experience, Butterball," Cal said in a voice that there was no arguing with. He recalled how he'd loved being in a tent at the Ransoms'.

"Cal, I'm not the survivor camp type."

"Yes, you are."

"Darling, what are you doing?" I asked Cal.

He'd taken off his shoe and was using it as a shovel.

"We need shelter. It's too cold to sleep on top of the sand," he said, sweat rolling down his face. "We have to sleep on the beach."

We both began digging to make a cave in the sand. I felt like we were climbing into a foxhole, but Cal seemed to be enjoying the whole experience. I confess, when the sun came up in the morning, it really was beautiful to be on the beach. I had taken off my high heels, and I felt this was just another childish adventure with Cal. Cal had sand all over his hair, between his fingers and sprinkled all over his clothes, and so did I. We climbed out of our foxhole.

When we arrived in New York, Cal wanted me to stay with him at East End Avenue. I hated arguments and I didn't want to disappoint him, but the incident at Fire Island made me want to go home and wash up and think about what I was getting into with my passion for Cal. I was still covered in sand when he dropped me off at my Park Avenue apartment. I was embarrassed when the elevator man tried very hard to avoid looking at me. Cal meanwhile was taking the car back to the rental place. I hoped he wouldn't kill himself or someone else on the way. He was a terrible driver. It was absurd but somehow funny. I had no idea that this was the beginning of the end of our romance and the beginning of Cal's manic insanity. It had been a trip to hell.

26

The Engagement Party

My friend Berta Salkind, a beautiful and very rich Mexican painter, came to visit me in New York. She was extremely exotic with dark hair and a marvelous smile. I believed her to be very talented. She painted in the style of Diego Rivera, and she had been one of my only friends during my past life in Paris. She was married to a billionaire film producer, Alexander Salkind, who would later go on to make the *Superman* movies. Berta often came to visit me in New York but didn't stay at my father's Park Avenue apartment. She stayed at the Pierre. Cal had telephoned me the day after our Fire Island experience to tell me he was giving a big party. He sounded very excited.

"What kind of party?" I asked.

"It's a surprise, but don't forget to dress up. I want to show you off to my friends."

"Do you mind if I invite one of my friends?"

"Of course not. Your friends are my friends," Cal said with his usual loving voice. "It's going to be a lot of fun. It's going to be held at the house of my good friend Blair Clark. He's now in the television business, and he has an elegant townhouse in Turtle Bay."

I invited Tom Guinzburg, publisher of Viking Press, a friend of mine, to come along with us. He was recently divorced and since, at the time, Berta was separated from her husband, I thought they might like meeting each other. Tom arrived at 6:30 to pick Berta and me up in his car, and we set out to Cal's party at Blair Clark's. I thought it was going to be a casual cocktail party of just about six people, but when we arrived at Blair Clark's townhouse and entered, I saw that a cocktail party with about thirty people was in full swing. Everyone was boisterous, drinking, eating, laughing, and gossiping. There were many people from the literary establishment, like Lionel Abel, a short, dark man who ran the *Partisan Review*. I saw, from the corner of my eye, my friend from the playwright unit of the actor's studio Norman Mailer, and talking with him I recognized novelist William Styron, whose novel *Lie Down in Darkness* had been a huge literary success in 1951.

Everyone was milling around trying to talk. This was so sweet of Cal to put all this together for me, I thought. Everyone loved him and admired his poetry. I saw a lot of poets I had met at the PEN Club and at the home of Oscar Williams, who had set up the poetry readings of Dylan Thomas before he died. I looked for James T. Farrell, but he wasn't there, and then I remembered that James and Dorothy had gone on a trip to Europe and weren't expected home until the next day. Cal came running over to me, excited and handsome as usual. He loved parties, I now realized, and he was so proud to introduce me to his literary friends. W. H. Auden was there. So were many other famous poets. I felt as if I were at the Century Club on steroids.

Cal seemed overexcited. I had no idea he was now in a manic state: I had never seen him like that before. Sweat was pouring down his face. I was standing and talking with Lionel Abel and Cal.

"Congratulations," Lionel Abel said to me as I looked around at the crowd.

"On what?" I asked innocently.

"Your engagement. This is your engagement party. Didn't Cal tell you?" he said, laughing so hard I could see his yellow teeth.

"This all comes as a surprise to me," I told Cal.

But I wasn't laughing. Lionel overheard me saying this to Cal. Lionel Abel came next to me.

"Oh, Cal did the same thing to Lizzie in Boston. Maybe it's Cal's way of having a good time. He loves to shock, and I'm sure nobody here knows you're not actually engaged," Lionel Abel said to us both with a drunken smile on his face as I looked at his disgusting yellow teeth...

I felt Cal might have at the very least consulted me. Outside of Berta and Tom, none of my friends were there, but I assumed Cal wanted me to meet his friends. As I milled around with my glass of champagne, I looked around to see that I was more or less a stranger at my own engagement party. I felt alone. Corks were popping like pistols. Cal threw his arms around me. I could hardly laugh now, since I could tell he'd been drinking. I didn't like it, but he was so animated and cheerful. I didn't want to sound like a nag by telling him he was drinking too much. He kept repeating over and over again, "We're engaged, we're engaged!" He was so happy. He was getting high on champagne. I was a bewildered Alice in this party, a complete wonderland. I was literally surrounded by famous, strange people talking jabberwocky talk that I couldn't understand. I tried to relax and fit in with the crowd of excited literary men and women I didn't know.

Everyone, especially Blair Clark, the waspy uptight host, seemed to be overwhelmed by Cal's charisma. After about an hour, some of the guests began to leave. Stanley Kunitz and Elise had given me a big kiss and left early. There were just a few people left. Cal and Bill Styron, whom I recognized from the dust jacket of *Lie Down in Darkness,* were soon talking in loud voices in the middle of the living room. Their voices rose in an argument. The few people who were left went silent and stared at them as they were arguing. Cal had often talked about his hatred of Stalin and how Stalin had murdered and imprisoned millions of his own citizens and tortured so many writers such as Pasternak, Solzhenitsyn, and Akhmatova.

He always talked about the fear that artists had under Stalin that they would be murdered, and he considered Stalin to be Mephistopheles. I could see that most people at the party were surprised to hear Cal screaming against Stalin at the top of his lungs. Everyone stopped talking to listen to Cal.

"Everyone who thinks Stalin is worse than Hitler, step behind me," Cal called out. "And those who think Hitler is worse, stand behind William Styron."

He was going mad. I didn't understand what was happening. Styron got very annoyed and walked off in a huff, dragging his wife with him. Everyone was shocked and nobody moved. Whatever kind of game Cal thought he was playing, nobody wanted to play it with him. I knew Cal had read all the testimony from the Nuremburg Trials, but I'd never heard him talk about Hitler. I began to cry. Cal was flipping out. He wasn't the Cal I knew. He was somebody else.

Before I knew it, I was the only person listening to this game of Simon says. Guests were putting on their coats quickly to leave the party. Berta was gone. Tom Guinzburg left without even saying good-bye to me. Oh, God—what was happening to my darling Cal? They must have all seen that Cal was acting in a strange way. I'd never seen him this way. It was so frightening. It was as if the guests heard lightning and ran to avoid the storm. Looking back, everyone at the party ran away in fear because they all knew about Cal's psychotic episodes. I was the only one at the party who knew *nothing* about his madness. I thought Nancy Tish was just jealous of me. I had never imagined that Cal would exhibit this weird behavior. Why was he this way? It was almost as if he was playing a part in a movie. It was as if he had become Adolf Hitler, but the only person left in the room was me. The butler was gone, the maids passing the finger foods had disappeared, and the guests were out the door. Blair Clark had run upstairs to his room. I stood there for what seemed like hours, watching Cal walking toward me. I felt a chill. I wanted to take Cal and go home.

I could not believe what he was doing. He was clicking his heels like a Nazi and goose-stepping toward me. Cal lunged at my throat, throwing me down on the floor. His face was white and empty. There was nobody there. In fact, for a few seconds, his face was completely empty. The angel was gone. Lucifer took the angel's place. Was this what insanity was? Was this delusional behavior? I had never experienced anything like this in my life. Where was my darling Cal?

"I'm Hitler, and you're a Jew, and I'm going to kill you," he said, putting his strong hands around my neck. I managed to lie still until he took his hands off my neck, and then he passed out. All I can remember is that he'd tried to choke me. He'd fallen to the ground in a psychotic or drunk fit, perhaps a combination of both. I'll never know. I had seen Blair Clark running up the stairs, but he was nowhere to be found. I tried to revive Cal. For a terrible moment, I thought he was dead.

"Help!" I screamed.

No one came. Blair Clark didn't come down the stairs. I only learned later that Blair Clark had seen these fits before, and he was afraid of Cal because Cal was very strong. I had to drag Cal up the stairs. The thought that he'd had a stroke crossed my mind. Forgetting about my fear, adrenaline kicked in. I pulled Cal along the floor and dragged him, up, up, painstakingly up Blair's stairs. On the second floor I managed to lift his heavy body off the floor and threw him on a narrow bed in the guest room. I'd never seen anything like this before. I saw he had an erection under his trousers, even while he was passed out. It made me think that sex and psychosis go together. I pulled the covers over him. Sweat was dripping from his body. His eyes were rolled up in his sockets, and he was in some terrible world of his own, behind the gates of some mysterious horror. I prayed that he wouldn't wake up and try to strangle me again. I just sat and cried at his side. I ran to Blair's room and screamed "help" over and over and banged on his door.

"Blair, please help—Cal's sick."

I banged on his bedroom door over and over, but Blair wouldn't come out to face this scene.

"Open the door! Cal is sick!" I screamed. "He's breathing too heavy. I don't know what to do!"

No Blair Clark. Cal was out cold and I was the only person in the room with him. Frightened, but afraid that Cal might actually die, I sat at his bedside all night. I prayed for him. I cried. I held his cold hands. I kissed his sweating face. About 4:00 in the morning, three friends who Blair Clark must have called came with an ambulance to put Cal in a straitjacket and take him to Presbyterian Hospital. They had all apparently been through this before. One of his friends, Professor Fred Dupee, who I had just met before the party and recognized from Columbia University, came up to me.

"I'm sorry for you," Fred said. "Please don't talk about this to anyone. We who love him don't want this to get out to anyone."

I wondered if Dupee knew that Cal had tried to choke me.

"I won't say anything," I said, but I was very shaken.

As the ambulance drove away, I hailed a cab and went back to my father's apartment. Aunt Jewel met me at the door. She could see that I was crying. I told her what had happened.

"It's not your fault," she said. "You had no way of knowing he was a very sick man. How would you know? He seemed very charming and perfectly normal to me."

"I was going to marry him," I sobbed. "I loved him so much."

"You'll get over this. It was not to be. By going mad, he did you a favor. It's better that you found this out now rather than later."

I felt tiny and small. I just wanted to disappear into the blankets and never wake up.

27

At the Farrells'

After Cal tried to strangle me, I stayed in bed at my father's house. I was in a state of shock for days. Finally I pulled myself together and realized that I felt deceived. Cal was, to say the least, not who I thought he was. Cal had promised me that we would have an incredibly luxurious and creative future, and there was no reason for me not to believe him. I was now repelled. He had polluted all my dreams. We had our life planned out as to where we would live, how many children we would have, even to the fact that Cal wanted me buried in Dunburton, New Hampshire in the Winslow family cemetery. I was now angry at myself, but also at James T. Farrell. He must have known that Cal was psychotic, delusional, and manic-depressive. Why hadn't he told me?

I went several days later to the Farrells' apartment on Broadway, sobbing and yet demanding to have the truth told to me. I felt hurt. I felt misery. I felt pain.

In memory, my brain was pulsating with everything I knew about the Farrells. James and Dorothy had divorced while James was writing a novel at the Colony of Yaddo. One day, James left Dorothy at Yaddo with Elizabeth Ames and other writers to march in a May Day parade. At that time he was a Communist sympathizer. At the parade he had gotten drunk and forgot all about Dorothy. Dorothy had fallen in love with James when she was sixteen, a rich young girl in Chicago. She had taken her college money to run off with him to Paris. She adored James and told me many of their Paris stories. She gave me insight into what Paris was like before the Second World War. The Farrells had socialized with Ernest Hemingway, who James got along with well enough for them to become close friends. They were also great friends with James Joyce, whose home they were invited to several times to hear Joyce, who was almost blind, sing his own poetry in his beautiful Irish tenor voice. James, Dorothy told me, hocked his typewriter when they went broke, but when money started pouring in from short stories he bought the typewriter back again. James had been her great love. Then, according to Dorothy, at the infamous May Day parade, James had met the beautiful red-haired actress Hortense. She became pregnant. He immediately divorced Dorothy and married Hortense. Very soon he was the father of two children, Kevin from Hortense and another child nobody knew about who was born mentally retarded and was put in an institution. Later he divorced Hortense, who had turned into a conceited shrew, and remarried Dorothy. Was she the mother of his crazy child? If she was, she never spoke about it. I remember, right after I met James, which was during my freshman year at Bennington, when I was seventeen and he was living alone, he often told me loving stories about his marriage with Dorothy, who had so unselfishly helped his career. Two years later, when I was a junior at Bennington, I received an invitation that read "Mr. and Mrs. James T. Farrell invite you to the wedding reception of Mr. and Mrs. James T. Farrell." They had re-married. They were both warm and loving to me. I loved them as much as I loved my parents. They were my literary parents. I once thought Dorothy might resent James T. Farrell's platonic admiration for a young girl who he so generously adopted as his protégée. But she adopted me as a surrogate daughter.

Dorothy often said I would be a great poet and had sent my manuscript of poems, written instead of a thesis at Bennington, to her good friend Malcolm Cowley, who was the Editor in Chief at Viking Press. Since I was only nineteen, Cowley said, "She is very talented but too young. Send it to us again when she is older." I loved James and Dorothy as if they were my literary parents. How could James and Dorothy not warn me about the nature of Cal's mental illness? I went inside their huge pre-war apartment on Broadway with a chip on my shoulder.

"James, Cal is crazy. He tried to strangle me after a party he gave for our engagement at the home of his friend Blair Clark."

"What happened?"

"Cal and Bill Styron got into a heated argument, 'Who was a worse monster, Stalin or Hitler?' and afterwards he thought he was Adolf Hitler. Everyone became afraid of him as they could see he was foaming at the mouth, sweating, and the entire party left. I stayed and he threw me down on the floor. While I was on the floor, he said he was Hitler and I was a Jew as he put his hands on my neck, and if I hadn't stayed just perfectly calm until he got up off my body and then passed out, I would have been murdered. Now I just found out from Stanley Kunitz he had done this before. Why didn't you tell me? Why didn't anyone tell me? How would I know he was a psychopath or whatever he is? I went to see his dumpy psychiatrist, Dr. Viola Bernard, and she never told me he was dangerous or even on Thorazine or lithium and he was schizophrenic or whatever he is. All she did was sort of interview me and tell me she felt he was happier than he was in any other time of his life, and I was good for him. I met all his friends, Stanley and Elise Asher, and they didn't tell me anything. Until now, neither did the Epsteins. Or Bob Silver. How would I know Cal was mentally ill? I don't move in literary circles. I met his friend Elizabeth Bishop when I was interviewing her for my thesis at Columbia. She never told me Cal was in and out of insane asylums or institutions."

"Of course not," James said sarcastically. "She's been in and out of institutions herself. It's a well-kept secret. It takes one to know one." He was very upset. "But honestly," James said, "I had no idea that Cal was violent. I only thought he was slightly mad. What happened at Yaddo should have given me a clue," James said guiltily.

"What happened?" I asked. James looked at Dorothy, and she told him he should spill the beans.

"Cal went to Yaddo to work on a memoir, and he got it into his head that Mrs. Ames, who ran Yaddo, was a Communist and that she had a longtime friend at Yaddo who was a member of the Communist Party. He went bananas because during his Catholic period he evolved into a Communist-hating Christian. He tried to get Mrs. Ames kicked out. He wrote letters. He marshaled all his friends who stayed there and I think a few people like Mary McCarthy and Elizabeth Hardwick, who he had just met and was having an affair with, took his side. But it caused an uproar and literally dozens of writers who had stayed at Yaddo loved Mrs. Ames. They wrote letters to the committee of admissions saying they wanted her to stay. Oh, they all wrote indignant letters, John Cheever, Saul Bellow, I remember almost everyone we knew signed letters to keep her. I think that those protest letters from his peers upset Cal terribly because many of his good friends, such as myself and Delmore Schwartz, took Mrs. Ames's side. I heard he went off to see Allen Tate and he became crazy again and had to be later hospitalized. But you know I'm not a gossip," James said. "I walk around in pajamas and all I think of is my writing. Last time I saw him at a conference, he seemed fine."

James sat in the living room. I saw his bright neon blue eyes under his thick Coke-bottle glasses. But now when he spoke it was with anger. "How dare he? I'll kill the prejudiced motherfucker."

Dorothy broke in. "James was always fond of Cal. They were at several literary conferences together, and they both hated Stalin and became anticommunists. They knew what Stalin did to writers. But believe me, James never would have encouraged you to interview Cal or even meet him in Cambridge years ago if he had any idea Cal was so mentally ill. Whenever we saw him, which was sometimes with the poets Marya and Horace Gregory, Cal was sweet and polite and a true gentleman. He did seem gloomy at times, but never grandiose or delusional. He sometimes looked burdened with anxiety. But what writer doesn't?"

Dorothy was now hugging me and kissing me. James made a drink. He had gone to his study to write. When I arrived, he saw me crying and he felt it was better to let me talk, woman to woman, to Dorothy. But now he was back.

"I had no idea he was still mentally ill," James said. "It was a well-kept secret."

"Of course it was," Dorothy said. "He had to earn a living. Harvard may be a liberal arts college, but they don't have lunatics teaching there."

"Oh, be quiet, Dorothy. Everyone teaching at Harvard is a lunatic. Maybe they put him in the loony bin once, but I never paid much attention. He was a great teacher, I was told, and he seemed so stable. However," James continued, "I thought it was strange that one day you went to interview him and the next day he left his wife and took an apartment. But my friend who teaches at Harvard told me he slept around with young girls plenty even though he was married to Elizabeth Hardwick. Dorothy and I felt two poets who fall in love do rather strange things.

"He even called me one day, I don't know if I told you, and thanked me for introducing him to you. He sounded perfectly sane to me. He said he loved your poetry, and he was grateful that I had helped you publish. He admitted he was in love. He asked me how we'd met, and I explained that when you were a freshman home from college on vacation, I was introduced to you by Mr. Marber, the manager of your father's hotel, where I was living. Your father, as you remember, didn't want us to meet and be literary buddies because he thought I was just an old man who drank too much and never paid his bills on time, which of course at that time was true. I told Sandra we would meet at a restaurant called Darby's Pickin' Chicken and discuss Flaubert. End of story.

"But the fact that he was delusional, that comes as a surprise. And that he believed he was Hitler, that is really amazing. Except, come to think of it, Dwight Macdonald—who is a real lefty and hates my guts but nonetheless is always asking me for favors—took me to lunch one day and said he had seen Cal and all he could talk about was Hitler. It seems that when he was in Holland with Lizzie, he sat for a year in a houseboat reading all the testimony of the Nuremburg Trials. And then Farrar & Straus sent me an advance copy of *Imitations*, and I saw the poem he translated of Montale about Hitler, and I thought it was excellent. There is no doubt Cal is the greatest poet in America. It's too bad he's so ill. You didn't give him any gifts, did you?" James asked. "Did he ever borrow money?"

"What do you mean, James? She doesn't have any money," Dorothy said.

"Well, whatever is in the East End Avenue apartment, you better take back right away," James said. He added with urgency: "You should never see him again. If he wants to continue the affair, you just have to use one word: *Never*. Let him go back to his wife. She can take care of him. I began to cry.

"Stop crying. You're too young to play nursemaid to a nut," James said. "Obviously Lizzie is good at that."

"Do you know what, James? I've been writing a poem called 'Ivory and Horn'; it's totally stream-of-consciousness and symbolic, but I'd like to read it to you."

"Darling, we would like nothing better," Dorothy said, giving me a whiskey and making herself one.

I took out my poem to read. I knew I felt safe being in the Farrells' home. It was filled with some of Dorothy's beautiful Irish furniture from the Butler family in Chicago. The Butler family was very wealthy. Dorothy claimed she remembered William Butler Yeats reading to her when she was a child at the foot of her bed in Chicago. Dorothy could sometimes have a terrible temper, and she could scream at Jim out of concern for his health. I often heard her screaming at him to stop drinking Scotch and milk and him telling her that "milk is good for you." She watched over his health, and he had turned into a less alcoholic man since they had remarried. When I first met him at the Dryden, he was often so drunk and thin that Mr. Marber told me that several times priests had come to his room to give him his last rites. Now he was writing seven hours a day, and he was truly a great friend.

"You know, James," I said, "remember the second year that I was back from Bennington and living at my father's hotel?"

"I remember," he said. "Read the poem. Read it loudly. I'm getting old and deaf."

I began reading "Ivory and Horn." I stood behind an old green velvet chair and meditated for a moment. In that moment I remembered the first reading I had ever given in my life right there in that living room at James and Dorothy's apartment. James was very active in the labor movement, and he had invited a lot of labor-movement men to their house. He was now anti-communist and like Cal hated Stalin, that was probably the basis of their friendship. Dorothy was a socialist, but they both gave money to the labor movement.

When I first gave a reading, I was nineteen and about to graduate from Bennington and had put together my first collection of poems, many of which James had helped me to publish. I wondered if they were too intellectual for the labor-movement crowd, but I gave in to James prompting me. I had read ten poems, and the applause of the men had surprised me. I realized I really enjoyed reading to an audience. And now, here I was, having just had a disastrous love affair that ended with Cal being a prisoner behind locked doors in Presbyterian Hospital. And I was reading again, to people who loved me and appreciated my poetry. I read the last part of the poem about Cal and me, "Ivory and Horn."

8
In the animal hospital:
Jaws of frightened animals. I looked at them,
Afraid to see the hairy cats completely shaved.

9
Near the tiger's bed, my eyes could see
Lovers dancing ceremoniously
Gracefully, along the corridor.
Geese in slippers danced the varnished floor
Lovingly, lovingly.

On the white pallor of varnishing,
Ladybirds and clock-o-clays could sing.
Bees spun music on the chrome
Of a basin's sun waxed honeycomb
And Jaguars pranced. A chittering toad
Sang to the blue eyes of a hog,
Lovingly.

Lovers, when at last from sweet content
You are caught in dreaming argument,
You will drowse in grass
Under the sea where swans are bound at last,
Lovingly, lovingly.

10

I would like back my jungle gifts, as I now
Understand they were given on the basis of being
Deceived. These gifts are:

One white Mexican bird of peace,
One silver and glass treasure box,
A golden ring,
My kaleidoscope,
One Japanese pen,
One Japanese ink grinder,
One Japanese scroll,
One small fan,
One book about the life of Mozart,
One red velvet crying pillow,
One picked-through book of Mallarme,
One straw angel,
Two geraniums,
Two pink tablecloths,
One white linen napkin,
Two small candleholders with peacocks on them,
Sugar tongs,
A blue holy book for the Holidays.

That is all that is necessary for me to say to you
At the present moment. I hope you enjoy tearing
My white nightgown and my white toothbrush.

11

I woke and sucked my thumb. My room
Had melted into stones.
Bookcases filled with books were filled with stones.
The dresser drawer was saddled with a stone.
Uneven stones, inviting all contours,
Were varnished on my pillow.
Stones in the mirror. Cinnabar and stone
You will find that I am
Ready for lapidation. I wept
And heard the bridegroom call my name

12

Then Angel Lucifer walked the wall
Past the living-room and down the halls
Into my bedroom. He rocked
Me to his fables.
I laid me down to sleep and blurred
My eyes upon his cackling bird. We flew
Into the underworld. My arms
Stuck to his bird's crest, fingers curled
Around his wings. And I was borne
Over the gates of Ivory and Horn.

"It's terrible that a beautiful young girl like you with such a big heart had to have such a ghastly experience. But we learn. We learn from everything," Dorothy said philosophically. "And now you have this heartfelt poem, 'Ivory and Horn,' to remind you forever of this experience, and to publish so that others who have experienced the same kind of tragedy will treasure your understanding of this insanity. The poem is Cal's gift to you."

"Some gift," James said sarcastically, helping himself to another drink.

28

In the Hospital

"Hurry up. I want you to see me," was all Cal could say over the phone.

He called every ten minutes. Was he psychotic now? Or was it over? "Who can tell us how to lead our lives?" kept going over in my brain. He sounded perfectly sane over the telephone. He was now manic, not delusional.

I agreed to visit him only because I held on to the hope of seeing the old Cal. I now realized that Cal's family and friends kept his schizophrenic delusions and manic-depressive states a secret. He hinted about it in his poetry, but I'd thought it was his imagination about what it would be like to be hospitalized. He had been loving. Dignified. Sexual. Brilliant. Creative. Reliable. And now this? What had cracked? His mind?

For months
My madness
Gathered strength
To roll all sweetness in a ball
In color tropical
Now I am frizzled, stale and small

Who knew this was the experience of Cal? After Cal was collected by a posse of his good friends and shunted to the loony ward of Presbyterian Hospital, Blair informed me, briefly and without any compassion in his voice, that he had been present at many episodes of Cal's "medical depressions, breakdowns, violent fits." Blair told me about the affair that Cal had had with a Washington socialite for six months while he was at the Library of Congress, and he had tried to choke her in a fit of violence that came out of nowhere. Oh, God, crazy Nancy had been telling the truth after all.

Cal was in the lock-up ward of Presbyterian Hospital for two months. He kept telephoning from the hospital every few hours, begging me to come and see him. His powers of recuperation were amazing. It was as if he were an alcoholic who had come out of a blackout and felt great because he didn't have a clue as to what had happened the night before. I had studied alcoholism, on my own, as I was never to forget that my mother's sister, my favorite Aunt Moll, who was beautiful and talented, had been an alcoholic and in the end been sent to Bellevue and then, when released, had taken her own life. I had read about memory stopping in the brain if one had too much to drink. When I saw Cal lying in his hospital bed in the Presbyterian Hospital, he was all smiles and charm. He gave me his grandfather's gold watch so I would come visit him on time. He still loved me. He had no memory of being violent or delusional. When he spoke to me on the phone three or four times a day, there was no sadness or shame. Even guilt was missing from his voice. Now I felt that Cal was a tormented soul out of the inferno of Dante I only had pity for him. Every day I woke up and I dressed in an old suit that was black and suitable. When I arrived at the hospital, Cal sat up in bed like a little child happy to have a visitor. I felt as if I weren't going to a hospital but going to a funeral.

Memories were hammering against my head. The hospital was so depressing. The bathroom smelled of piss and feces. There was a smell of formaldehyde in the air. It was like a nightmare. When Cal sat up, I could see that some of his friends had brought him books, and there was the photograph of me in the frame next to his bed, a photograph he loved that sat on his desk in the East End Avenue apartment and now sat in the loony bin. He held in his hand the tiny gold pocket watch he wanted me to keep.

"This belonged to my grandfather Lowell," he said proudly. "I want you to have it as another engagement present."

I took the watch and knew that I would keep it as a remembrance of this love affair, which I now knew was over. I could never risk my life again.

I knew at that moment our relationship, our love affair, our engagement was a terrible hoax. Now I wanted to use my best efforts to persuade Cal to go back to his wife and child, and that would give him the recuperative powers he needed and the home that could stabilize him. I told him that every time I visited him, which was once a day at his insistence. Often Dr. Bernard came to visit him and medicate him with Thorazine, a drug I knew nothing about. I was in despair. But I was also angry. I had burned my bridges with Ivry. What was I to do?

I kept thinking, as I sat for hours in the hospital, of Lowell's *Life Studies,* which I had bought in Paris when it came out in 1959. The book was confessional, even though Cal denied this. It came, in many ways, out of Cal's experiences, and many young poets including myself were struck by its courage to not only reveal secrets but to take the banality of evil and the personal and twist them into poetry. Each time I visited him at the hospital, Cal was begging me over and over to not abandon him. Lizzie never came to the hospital. Neither did Jason Epstein. Or Blair Clark. But I sat there every day for two hours.

Now Cal was the killer king in my eyes. He was pleading with me to come back to the hospital every day. He seemed normal again. The drugs from Dr. Bernard must have tamed him. "I love you, Butterball," he said. It broke my heart. I smiled all day and cried all night.

"I'm in a centerless flux," he said over the phone.

He sounded so sad, it broke my heart. It is possible he had even forgotten his delusional Hitler episode. It had been so real, I tried not to think of it. I never told anyone.

"I'm feeling music-mad," he told me. "Can you bring me some classical records? I'm allowed to listen to my own music on a phonograph."

I brought him different operas. Also recordings of Bach, Mozart, Schumann, Schubert, Brahms. Dr. Bernard was there, constantly trying out new medications. Lithium hadn't been invented yet for manic-depression and, poor woman, she was trying her best. Meanwhile, he was taking pills that might have been snake oil.

"I'll bring you *The Creation*," I told him.

He had felt so exalted by the music when he went to the concert at Carnegie Hall, I hoped the music would act as therapy. I kept turning over and over in my mind that Cal had once told me that his late mother, Charlotte, had been an assistant to the psychiatrist Merrill Moore in Cambridge and later became a person who saw some of his patients herself, dispensing practical advice even as she didn't have any medical or psychiatric training. Cal told me she had said, "I've consulted with Jung and he says your symptoms are schizophrenic." She had gone to Switzerland to see the great dream specialist, dragging her husband with her, in a quest, no doubt, to understand her only son and his disturbing behavior. Was Dr. Bernard's diagnosis a fraud? Was he schizophrenic, not manic-depressive? No one knows or will ever know.

But in 1961, I realized that nobody had a clue as to what triggered Cal's madness. Was it chemical? Wires in the brain confused and unplugged? Was it a reaction to feeling like a little Napoleon in his childhood? There were all these experts in the mental ward of a first-rate hospital, but what did these doctors really know about madness? About schizophrenia? About depression? About mania? About poetry? About art? It seemed to me more and more that Cal connected sex with power, but why did that make him ill? And why did just sitting quietly with me on a bench looking at the East River make him so sweet and sane?

As I sat in the Neurological Institute at the Columbia Presbyterian Medical Center, I resolved to break off with Cal immediately. He had been there two months. One had to visit him by being led through two sets of locked doors. But now in the hospital Cal seemed to be filled with energy. He was smoking his packs of cigarettes. Surrounded by smoke, he was stuffing chocolates into his mouth and smiling at me as if he were still to become my husband. He also talked about himself in connection with Hart Crane, Alexander the Great, and Pasternak. It was pitiful. I couldn't tell what could happen, or what I should do. Would he come out of this? Was my leaving him going to make him worse?

One of the people that Cal entertained at the medical center, while sitting up in his bed in his pajamas wearing a big smile, was Stanley Kunitz. One afternoon, Stanley took me aside in one of the visiting rooms. He talked to me like a Dutch uncle. His huge brown eyes that had formerly twinkled were sad.

"Listen, Sandra, you're a young girl. Cal is a very sick man. He is never going to get any better. He is only going to get worse. You're young enough to run away from all of this. That is my advice. Run for your life."

With sadness, I went for a walk with Cal the next week in the hospital gardens. Cal took my hand as if we were still lovers.

"Never leave me," he said.

"I am leaving you," I said.

"No. No."

"Cal. You have to go back to your wife. She will take care of you. She loves you and she is your wife. I cannot go on seeing you."

"Never, never. Please, I love you. Marry me." He looked at me with tears. "I want to be with you for the rest of our lives," he said.

He pretended he didn't understand that I was leaving him. I was crying too. This, I thought, was a final parting.

"I know, dear, but it's not to be."

I walked him back to the hospital, and I hoped that would be the end.

"Marry me, Butterball," he said.

"Never," I said. "It's not to be."

"Please don't say never," he said. "We can spend the rest of our lives together."

I was crying so hard, I felt faint.

He kept repeating the words "never, never" as I left the hospital.

Cal never stopped calling me. Two years later, he visited me. My father had died. I was living alone at 3 East 78th Street. He was nicely dressed and wore a tie, but he was not Cal. He was someone else. All the energy he'd once had was gone. He was to me a broken light bulb. He was flat.

"My book, *Manhattan Pastures,* just won the Yale Younger Poets Award," I told him.

"I'm on lith," he said, as if he didn't hear me.

No joy. His eyes, which were cat's eyes, filled with tears. "Will you send me your book?" he asked.

"Yes," I said.

He kept calling. I didn't want to see him. I had divorced Ivry and had won the Yale Younger Poets Award. I was teaching. I finally answered his letter and calls by sending him my second book, *Manhattan Pastures*. Here is one of the letters he sent me.

April 28, 1963

Dear Sandra:

I did call up the other Wednesday evening, found you were out, and read the weather sign, I think, correctly, and desisted, for certainly I have no desire to add my boisterous confusion to your life. Or whatever it is I would add. Let me say I mean well and am really very fond of you.

I've now done my homework on Manhattan Pastures. *Probably I am too close to judge. Anyhow, they make quite a different impression from your Paris volume. There's the old freshness, the city detail, the image from nowhere that entrances me, and I think must be in the style of a later poetry. The style is simple and unrhetorical, but the images shy away from the logic and monotony of memories and the spatially possible. This gives a kind of freedom, and must have a great future. It's alien, though attractive to me, and I have even rather lamely tried in few things in this line, taking off from Wallace Stevens, rather than Neruda and some of the later French poets. Well, there's no keeping up, and after a while I think one settles for developing the undeveloped pointers in one's past style and experience. One tries to throw the stones out of one's garden, and no doubt turns up new ones. The poems I like best in your volume are mostly old favorites: "Cannon Hill," "Clay and Water," "Paris Acropolis," and probably, with a little wincing, "Ivory and Horn."*

I see I never got to saying how this book is different from your other. I think it's in its being longer and larger, and mostly avoiding your earlier rather chopped cuteness. What next? Rereading your very touching poem about your father, I'd say what you might want to attain is a bit more structural body, and oddly enough a larger, free-er push into the real story. But the book's delightfully you and varied.

And you too, dear, go on being you and fresh and changing. Let there be peace and a long lifetime for you!

Love,

Cal

29

Caroline

Cal divorced Lizzie and married Caroline Blackwood. All the world knew by now that Cal was mentally ill, and the fact that he was able to work as a professor, teaching in England, was a miracle. He continued, as did his friends, to cover up his psychotic attacks. It was ironic that Cal, who had once read Hart Crane's poem *The Bridge* to me on the Brooklyn Bridge, was now, to borrow from the poem, a Bedlamite himself. At one institution, after he dumped Lizzie for his second wife, Caroline, I had been told, he took a knife and started cutting and stabbing the padded walls. How he got the knife was a mystery. While he was with Caroline, he was committed five or six times to mental hospitals. Mental illness was as terrible as, if not more terrible than, physical illness. It is a mysterious curse. Caroline, I heard, couldn't handle his breakdowns. I heard that she constantly screamed at him, and he left her to go back to Lizzie.

Cal wrote to me constantly even after his third marriage to Caroline. I also went to London when my volume of collected poems *Earthworks* was published there. I visited Cal and his new wife while I was there. I had the feeling they had been arguing but were being civil because I was present. I felt sorry for Caroline. For Cal. For Lizzie. For his child.

30

Visit with Lizzie

Cal had begged me in letters to visit him in London. We were all to go to lunch. Would I please join him and his wife Caroline for lunch? At the lunch, Cal hardly ate any food. Cal was complaining about having to take a long trip in order to teach, and he was in a hurry to leave for the train. He was a total stranger. As for Lady Caroline Freud Citkowitz Lowell, I was shocked to see how badly she treated Cal. To me, it seemed she was on some kind of drugs. She was really doped up and had a Madonna face but was lacking in any animation. She looked angry at him. I couldn't wait to excuse myself. That was the last time I saw Cal, sitting with Caroline, his third wife. I could tell she was bewildered by all the Cals. The depressed Cal, the out-of-control delusional Cal. The man who seemed as depressed as he was.

Years later, I received a phone call. It was from Elizabeth Hardwick, Cal's ex-wife, inviting me for tea after I had seen Cal and Caroline again, surprisingly enough. Lizzie and I had several friends in common, and she was so sweet on the phone that I decided she must have wanted to talk to me very badly just to ring me, an old enemy, out of the blue, since we had never met. I had followed the literary gossip and the whole brouhaha of Cal taking her letters of anger, taping her phone calls where she begged him to come back to her and not marry Caroline, and weaving them together with taped conversations of other screaming phone calls, into poems that won him a second Pulitzer Prize. But that was Cal's *noblesse oblige,* stealing lines for poems wherever he could find them, even if they were from Lizzie's desperate phone calls. In his head he believed that he could do anything he wanted for the sake of immortality. In the end, what difference would humiliating Lizzie make as long as the poems were brilliant? But Lizzie Lowell didn't feel that way. She was mad as hell.

I remarked, "This is a really beautiful apartment, Lizzie."

She looked to me like a character out of a Tennessee Williams play, a combination perhaps of Stella and Blanche. Her makeup was very heavy. She was desperately trying to look young.

"I think a woman needs a nice setting, don't you?" she said to me.

My God, I thought, that was even a line out of a Tennessee Williams play.

So I was in her setting. During tea she turned to me and with a voice that had such anger she was almost like a primitive animal, she drawled in her Kentucky Southern accent: "I hate the one who's with him now. I hate her." She couldn't even say Caroline's name.

By "the one," I knew she meant Lady Caroline. I said nothing.

238

"I wished he had stayed with you. You're at least nice. Cal told me you are a wonderful person and very clean. You cleaned his house and washed and ironed his shirts. You took good care of him. You cut his hair. Cooked for him. This one is a filthy pig. I couldn't believe when I went to visit, how filthy she is." There was a silence, then she said with resignation, "Well, at least I knew him when he was young and beautiful."

No. No. I felt as if I was in a play, either by Oscar Wilde or by Euripides with Elizabeth Lowell, now my best friend. My heart broke for all the people who had loved Cal. Most of all, my heart broke for Elizabeth Lowell. I wanted to take her in my arms and hug her for all the braveness she had shown, and so I did just that. Soon tragedy turned to comedy. We laughed, two rivals, now friends.

A few years later, Cal left Lady Caroline to go back to Lizzie. Cal died of a heart attack in a taxicab in front of Lizzie's 67th Street apartment in 1977. He was coming back from visiting Sheridan, his son by Caroline, in England. As he sat in the taxi, Lizzie ran down to him, but it was too late.

He was dead. In his hands, wrapped in brown paper, was a portrait of Lady Caroline by her ex-husband Lucian Freud. What irony. What grief for poor Lizzie who gave poor Cal the only stability he ever had. What grief for us all to lose one of the great poets of the Western world.

31

Epilogue to a Love Affair

What I discovered while writing this love story was how naïve, gullible, and foolish I was at twenty-five, to have not seen the signs of Cal's insanity. It was obvious to almost everyone but me that Cal had mental problems. When I mentioned that I was seeing him to my friend, Alexandra, who knew many of the people he knew in the socialite set of Boston and New York, she said, "I've heard he is bonkers." I should have listened to her comment and taken it seriously. The fact was, there was not to be a happy ending to our love affair. To later find out that after Cal went back to Elizabeth he ran off again with several other women, promising to marry them, and then freaking them out by going insane and having to be incarcerated by his friends or Elizabeth over and over again was disturbing enough. But when a great celebrity poet is as charming as Cal, it is easy to deny his other self. His ability to recuperate and change back to his old self lasted until he married his third wife, and then his breakdowns and delusions became more and more frequent, more and more violent. When he was married to Caroline Blackwood and living in England, he hated teaching, since he did not command the respect that he did at Harvard. Ironically, the young English students he taught were more and more interested in Allen Ginsberg and Gregory Corso than they were in Robert Lowell. The raw food poets became popular and the cooked food poets became less known and less respected. And yet I feel that Randall Jarrell's prediction that "Robert Lowell would be read as long as people read English" will prevail. It doesn't matter whether he is read on paper or on a machine. His voice will always, in my opinion, be the genuine voice of America's greatest poet.

Many years later, I was fortunate to be treated by the great psychiatrist Dr. David Beres, the former head of the New York Psychoanalytic Institute. Unlike Cal's psychologist, who was a Thorazine pill pusher and, in my opinion, a very unsympathetic woman (Elizabeth agreed with me), Dr. Beres was able to make me aware that I had the emotional development of a girl of thirteen, which accounted for my gullibility then and, I'm afraid, now. Like most of the artists and poets I have met, most of whom are addicts, bipolar, manic-depressive, eccentric, or simply mad, I now know what Dr. Beres was saying about me could be said about almost every other artist I've ever known. We are all drunk on something. In Cal's case, I was drunk on his sexual attentions, his genius, and even his madness. The work remains, and even his aristocratic background—which had given him his manners and his dignity as a gentleman—will always be remembered by me with love. And yet, many years later, I realize that our love affair was a trauma that would never disappear. I read recently that the Japanese survivors of the atom bomb called the explosion of the bomb the *perkadom* or the flash-bang. The survivors said if you see the *perka*, you have a few seconds to dodge the *dom* which is on its way. Cal's going mad was the perka of this experience, not unlike the experience of an atom bomb. The survivors of the atom bomb said they could smell the burning flesh, which was like the smell of squid. Luckily I was able to run away from the perka and avoid the dom. Wounded forever, I still was able to survive.

Who cares if the nineteenth-century poet John Clare was mad? His home is enshrined in England because we just care that he was a great poet. The same may be said of Robert Lowell who became, for a short time, my beloved Cal. We are lucky to know him now through his work, as he left behind so many plays, so many poems, so many shards of value. It is my hope that wherever Cal is, he is in the place of the perfect mind of God, where his disease of madness is healed. I hope he is in those clouds where good men meet their fate, and when he walks he is walking on the verge of heaven.

CPSIA information can be obtained
at www.ICGtesting.com
Printed in the USA
BVOW04s2036240517
484590BV00008B/3/P